AREA CHILD PROTECTION COMMITTEES

To Sue, Tecka and Feni, and to Natasha, Huw and Gwyn

Area Child Protection Committees

ROBERT SANDERS
and
NIGEL THOMAS
Department of Social Policy and Applied Social Studies
University of Wales, Swansea

Ashgate

Aldershot • Brookfield USA • Singapore • Sydney

Published by
Ashgate Publishing Ltd
Gower House
Croft Road
Aldershot
Hants GU11 3HR
England

Ashgate Publishing Company
Old Post Road
Brookfield
Vermont 05036
USA

British Library Cataloguing in Publication Data

Sanders, Robert
    Area child protection committees. - (Welfare and society)
    1.Children - Services for - Great Britain 2.Abused children
    - Services for - Great Britain
    I.Title II.Thomas, Nigel
    362.7'0941

Library of Congress Catalog Card Number: 97-73609

ISBN 1 85972 613 5

Printed and bound by Athenaeum Press, Ltd.,
Gateshead, Tyne & Wear.

Contents

Figures and Tables

Acknowledgements

We would like to express our gratitude to Lawrence Conway at the Welsh Office for giving us the opportunity to be involved in the two studies which are featured in this book. We want to acknowledge as well the time and good will which was extended to us by all of those members and chairs of Area Child Protection Committees who helped us along the road to a better understanding of ACPCs. *Diolch yn fawr i bawb.* Above all we would like to acknowledge our indebtedness to Professor Sonia Jackson, who was the lead author of *Protecting Children in Wales* and who has helped us enormously with this book.

Introduction

Although forms of concern about cruelty to children have a longer history, child abuse as a central focus of child welfare services is very strikingly a phenomenon of the last thirty years. During that time it has gone from the discovery of 'baby-battering' to the contemporary preoccupation with sexual abuse in its various manifestations, and the professional energy, heartache and sheer resources expended on it have expanded at a rate that at times seems exponential. In most economically modernised countries child protection is now the predominant concern of the organisations providing welfare services to children and families.

Although a similar process has taken place all over the world, different countries and continents have each had their own distinctive emphasis. To some extent these variations probably reflect different patterns of abuse and different attitudes to children; but they also reflect widely differing styles of professional intervention, and widely differing views of the relationship between families and the state. The pattern in most of the English-speaking world has been to adopt to varying extents a *policing* response, as opposed to the predominantly *therapeutic* response seen in some European countries. It has also been to lay great stress on the importance of professions working together. In some cases, for instance in the United States, this has included mandatory reporting of suspicions of abuse.

The United Kingdom has not adopted mandatory reporting, at least in legal terms. What it has done, uniquely as far as we know, is to regulate quite formally the arrangements for inter-professional collaboration in response to child abuse or allegations of child abuse. Since the early 1970s agencies concerned with the health, welfare education and protection of children have been directed by central government to establish formal arrangements for regular interagency collaboration at both practitioner and managerial levels. The detail with which this has been specified has tended to increase in the intervening years, as procedures have been tightened in response to incidents and scandals. We summarise this history later in this chapter. However, our principal concern in this book is to examine how Area Child Protection Committees, as they have been known for ten years now, currently operate and to reach some estimation of their effectiveness.

Since this approach to protecting children has been in a sense an experiment with the United Kingdom as the laboratory, we hope that readers in other countries will be interested in its results. We do not claim that ours is the last word on the successes or failures (for we think there are both in good measure) of the experiment. It would be fairer to say that it is the first; for surprisingly little has been written about this peculiarly British approach to the problem of ensuring that diverse professions work together to protect children.

Purposes of this book

When one considers the wealth of literature that has accumulated in the general field of child abuse and child protection, it is startling that so little has been written specifically about the structures for managing services to protect children. Apart from the recent work of Christine Hallett and Elizabeth Birchall (Hallett and Birchall, 1992; Hallett, 1993; Birchall and Hallett, 1995; Hallett, 1995) there is very little published material. Indeed, to achieve their excellent review of the literature on coordination and child protection, Hallet and Birchall (1992) had to draw extensively on evidence of interagency coordination from other settings. This lack of emphasis in the literature on interagency working in child protection is all the more surprising if one considers the extent to which the changes in child protection, many of which have been initiated as a result of child fatality inquiries, have largely been directed at changing the structures of interagency work and attempting to get agencies to communicate more easily and with less friction. The barriers to agencies working well together have been known for many years (Norton and Rogers, 1981; Broskowski et al, 1982; Hallett and Birchall, 1992).

In Britain, the principal mechanism for ensuring that the management of child protection services is achieved on an interagency basis is through the operation of Area Child Protection Committees (ACPCs). These are multi-agency forums attended by senior managers from a range of organisations involved with children and families. If little has been written about the management of child protection services, even less has been written about Area Child Protection Committees. What literature exists is sometimes based on a misunderstanding of what it is that Area Child Protection Committees actually do; Lyon and de Cruz (1993, p.147) and Williams (1992) both appear to suggest that the ACPC directs the management of particular cases. In fact the main tasks of the ACPC have been clearly defined in *Working Together under the Children Act 1989* (Home Office et al, 1991):

    (a)   To establish, maintain and review local inter-agency guidelines on procedures to be followed in individual cases;

    (b)   To monitor the implementation of legal procedures;

    (c)   To identify significant issues arising from the handling of cases and reports from inquiries;

    (d)   To scrutinise arrangements to provide treatment, expert advice and inter-agency liaison and make recommendations to the responsible agencies;

    (e)   To scrutinise progress on work to prevent child abuse and make recommendations to the responsible agencies;

(f)   To scrutinise work related to inter-agency training and make recommendations to the responsible agencies;

(g)   To conduct reviews required under Part 8 of this Guide;

(h)   To publish an annual report about local child protection matters.

(*Working Together under the Children Act 1989*, para 2.12)

In Appendix 5 of *Working Together under the Children Act 1989* it is suggested that the membership of Area Child Protection Committees should comprise representatives of the following agencies:

a) Social work agencies
- Social Services Departments
- NSPCC (where active)

b) Health Authority
- District Health Authority management
- Medical and psychiatric services professionals
- Nursing

c) Family Health Services Authority
- FHSA management
- General practitioner representative of the local medical committee(s)

d) Education
- Local Education Authority (LEA)
- Teacher (normally a head)

e) Police

f) Probation

g) Armed services

This book attempts to examine the operation of ACPCs at more length than has been done hitherto. Its starting point is a detailed study of the effectiveness of ACPCs which we undertook in 1994 for the Welsh Office. As we explain in the next chapter, the study was based largely on talking to members of ACPCs. Many members of ACPCs are well placed to comment on the interrelationship between policy and practice. They may be the managers with the principal responsibility for directing child protection work in their own agencies; while as ACPC delegates they are charged with ensuring that their agencies work together with others to deliver coherent policies, and to some extent with determining what those policies are. Evans and Miller (1992) comment that 'ACPCs have grown both in size and the range of activities they undertake. They began life as forums designed to enable interagency discussions on matters of child protection policy and procedures. They are now used as major avenues through which governments implement their policies and guidelines.'

We make no apologies for relying in this book on research which was conducted in Wales. First of all, child protection services in Wales are certainly worthy of study in their own right. Secondly, they are as typical of the British context as anywhere else would be. Similar research to ours could have been based on a sample of areas or on one region such as the South East or North West of England, as other research has been. By working in Wales we have been able to study a whole country, with all the regional variations, mixture of urban and rural settings, differences in size and culture of professional agencies, that this implies. Certainly professional practice in Wales has its own particular idiosyncrasies and its own particular problems, preoccupations and blind spots; but then so does professional practice anywhere else. In a sense only the atypical can ever be really typical.

Moreover the same legislation applies in Wales as in England, and the same political context and the same general approach to child protection exist as in the rest of the UK. This means that the general conclusions from our research certainly have application throughout Britain. We think there are implications for North America and Australasia as well, where the system has some very similar characteristics and is based on some very similar assumptions. It may be that in continental Europe people have found other ways of protecting children that do not suffer from some of the drawbacks we have found; to establish that would require very different research from what we have been able to do. The book is not as wide ranging as we would have wished; we would have liked to devote more attention to international comparisons and also to some of the philosophical questions about child protection. However, the constraints of publishing deadlines and other commitments made that impossible. It is nearly three years now since we carried out the bulk of the research reported here (although other parts are much more recent). It is time to put it into the public domain and let others make what they will of it.

The development and function of Area Child Protection Committees

The predecessors of Area Child Protection Committees, the former Area Review Committees were set up following guidance on 'Non-Accidental Injury to Children' issued in April 1974 (Department of Health and Social Security, 1974b) shortly before the publication of the Maria Colwell Inquiry report (Department of Health and Social Security, 1974a). Dingwall, Eekelaar and Murray (1983) point out, however, that the background to the Area Review Committees can be traced back some thirty or so years to the Coordinating Committees set up in the early 1950s under a joint circular ... 'to secure the co-operation of all local statutory and voluntary agencies concerned with the welfare of children' including cases of neglect and ill-treatment, (p. 127).

The 1974 Guidance, in addition to recommending the introduction of registers and case conferences, 'strongly recommended ... urgent joint action' to set up committees either based on local authority or health authority boundaries, including senior representatives from both the statutory and voluntary sector agencies involved with children and their families. The primary purpose of such bodies was the joint development of policy in relation to 'local practices and procedures to be followed in the detailed management of cases'. A number of other functions were also recommended for Area Review Committees, including approving written instructions outlining the duties of workers, reviewing the work of case conferences, collecting information about the work being done, providing education and training, and considering ways to inform the general public about the role of various professionals whenever they are concerned about children being ill treated.

By the end of 1974, Area Review Committees had been established across England and Wales (Parton, 1991). In 1976, further guidance was issued by the Department of Health and Social Security ('Non Accidental Injury to Children: Area Review Committees'), which attempted to answer queries raised by the 1974 guidance. It advised that areas that had not established a register should do so, re-emphasised the value of case conferences, and stressed the importance of keyworkers in cases of non-accidental injury. By 1976, all areas had established Area Review Committees, with case conference systems and registers.

Because of concerns expressed by the police about not being informed when cases came to light, further Department of Health and Social Security guidance (1976) emphasised the importance of cooperation and advised that police representatives should be invited to both case conferences and Area Review Committees.

Following research by the British Association of Social Workers (BASW, 1978) into the variations in registrations between different areas, the Department of Health and Social Security issued guidance (1980) about the use of registers. Just as in the late 1960s and 1970s an initial emphasis on the 'battered-baby syndrome' had widened to encompass other forms of 'non-accidental injury', the 1980 guidance further broadened the range of situations to be covered by what were now called child abuse procedures. On this occasion severe and persistent neglect, and emotional abuse, were added to the list. (Sexual abuse was not considered to be a form of abuse in its own right at this stage, and was not included under the procedures unless accompanied by some other form of abuse.)

There followed a period of relative inactivity in terms of government guidance, until the Jasmine Beckford inquiry (London Borough of Brent and Brent Health Authority, 1985). Following the inquiry, and to some degree influenced by the BASW document, *The Management of Child Abuse* (BASW, 1985), the Department of Health and Social Security issued further guidance in draft form (Department of Health and Social Security, 1986). Agencies and individuals were asked to reply to the draft by Autumn 1986, creating an expectation that the document would be published during 1987. During 1987, however, events in Cleveland again called seriously into question the ability of different agencies to work together to protect children, and suggested that children could be put at additional risk of 'system abuse' by the failure of agencies to collaborate. These events delayed the publication of the new guidance pending the outcome of the Butler-Sloss Inquiry in 1988, and it did not eventually appear until later that year, under the title *Working Together*. In the view of Eaton (1988) however, there was nothing new about a lack of cooperation between agencies, and much of what was in the new guidance was already known before the Cleveland crisis.

Working Together introduced a number of changes of which the most important were: (1) the redesignation of child abuse intervention as 'child protection', and of Area Review Committees as Area Child Protection Committees; and (2) the formal identification of social services departments (SSDs) as lead agency. It did not give SSDs the power to make demands on other agencies for compliance with clearly accepted and understood accountabilities and responsibilities in child protection.

5

However the 1988 guidance did include much more sharply-defined expectations of local procedures manuals, especially in relation to investigative processes, case conferences and registers.

In 1991 revised guidance was issued as *Working Together Under the Children Act 1989*, both to take account of the new legal and philosophical framework of the Act and to reflect changes in child protection practice which had taken place in the three years since the publication of the first *Working Together* document. Among other things, the new guidance created an increased expectation of participation by families in the child protection process. It also for the first time gave guidance on dealing with organised abuse, and abuse by professionals. Both of these issues had come to prominence with the investigations in Orkney and Rochdale, and a succession of scandals in residential schools, children's homes and foster homes, which continue to the present time with the judicial inquiry into abuse of children in homes in North Wales. The new version also expanded and elaborated the functions of ACPCs; in particular, the remit was extended for the first time to include 'treatment'. In practice, however, ACPCs give very little consideration to issues around the post-trauma needs of abused children. The main body of the business of Area Child Protection Committees, as we will see, is taken up with procedures for the investigation of individual incidents of child abuse.

Outline of this book

It may be helpful to indicate how the following chapters are organised. Chapter 1 briefly describes the Welsh Office review: its aims, its methodology and its principal conclusions. There then follow two chapters focused on child protection policy: Chapter 2 looks at how child protection policy is understood by those charged with implementing it through the Area Child Protection Committees; while chapter 3 examines how those committees go about turning policy into practice in their constituent agencies. Chapter 4 focuses on the members of an ACPC: who they are, how they are recruited, and how they go about representing their agencies on the committee. Chapter 5 looks at the functioning of the committee *as a committee*: how meetings are conducted and agendas determined, and at the involvement of different agencies in the work of the committee. Chapter 6 presents a detailed examination of the procedures handbooks which are such an important product of the Area Child Protection Committees' work, and chapter 7 brings together some of our findings concerning the effects of reorganisation on the work of the committees.

The remaining chapters represent work done since we completed the Welsh Office review. Chapter 8 discusses the reviews of serious cases conducted under Part 8 of *Working Together*, and is based in part on work done recently by one of us with two other colleagues. Chapter 9 is an account of an attempt to widen the scope of interagency collaboration through the introduction of 'children's services plans'. Finally, chapter 10 draws together some of the recurring themes of the book and attempts to set them in a wider context.

Textual note

Area Child Protection Committees are sometimes referred to in full, but perhaps more often by their acronym of ACPCs. Sometimes when it helps the flow of the text, we call them simply 'committees' or on occasion 'the main committee' (as distinct from a subcommittee). We trust that the reader will understand these references. Also to ease the flow of reading, we refer to our report *Protecting Children in Wales* (Jackson, Sanders and Thomas, 1994) by its short title, or on occasion as the 'Welsh Office Review', (as in the title of chapter 1) without including a reference on each occasion. Finally, although there was a previous version of government guidance called *Working Together* (Department of Health and Social Security, 1988), reference to the currently operative guidance *Working Together Under the Children Act 1989* (Home Office, Department of Health, Department of Education and Science, Welsh Office, 1991) will simply be given in the text as '*Working Together*'; which is how it is normally referred to by those working in child protection.

1   The Welsh Office Review

In November 1993 the Welsh Office invited tenders for a review of the effectiveness of child protection policy in Wales, with the following terms of reference:

1. To report on how the Department's child protection policy is understood and interpreted by ACPCs;

2. To assess the contribution of Welsh ACPCs towards the implementation of Welsh Office policy;

3. To examine the level of resources made available to the ACPCs in particular to identify the source and amount of ACPC funds and the implications of any resource constraints for 2 above;

4. To identify those aspects of ACPC arrangements and practice in Wales that contribute most to ACPC effectiveness and its corollary ie those issues which present most difficulty: both these areas to be looked at in particular relation to interagency collaboration

5. To examine the ACPC's role and contribution to the development of child care policies in its geographical area of responsibility;

6. In the light of its findings, to make recommendations.

In guidance notes attached to the terms of reference it was specified that:

... fulfilment of the terms of reference will necessitate examination of ACPC structures; their priorities; their relationships with the Department; their constituent agencies and the community; their approach to joint working; their data requirements and collection; their management of tasks; their budgets; their strategy for dealing with the media and their training and evaluation procedures.

The successful tender was submitted by the Department of Social Policy and Applied Social Studies at the University of Wales Swansea, and the subsequent study was designed and carried out by the present authors under the direction of Professor Sonia Jackson, Head of the Department. Between us we had the experience of serving on an (English) Area Child Protection Committee and of working with all the eight Welsh counties; we therefore looked forward to doing the work and had a great deal of curiosity about what we would find.

On the other hand, we knew that we had very limited time and resources to complete the review. The report was required by the following March, and the short time period combined with the effect of competitive tendering meant that we would have to do all the work ourselves in addition to continuing to honour our teaching commitments. The methods we adopted reflect these constraints. Work began at the end of November 1993 and was eventually completed in April 1994, with a short extension to allow for some further work which became necessary during the course of the study (see below).

How the review was designed

The detailed design of the review was worked out by us on the basis of our discussions with a commissioning group at the Welsh Office. This group included representatives of the Area Child Protection Committees (ACPCs) as well as officials and advisory staff at the Welsh Office. The commissioning group was helpful in giving us guidance on priorities for the review; it also had an editorial role in relation to our final report, which it had the opportunity to see in draft form.

We decided to use two principal sources of evidence: documents and interviews. First, we studied a range of policy documents produced by the government and the ACPCs, together with the local procedures handbooks in each area and a sample of minutes of meetings and other records. Second, we arranged to carry out a series of semi-structured interviews with a sample of the members of each committee, and later on with the chairperson of each committee. We realised that we did not have the time or the resources to interview either the practitioners who operate child protection policy in individual cases or the families who are on the receiving end of services; had we done so, our conclusions might of course have been very different. This was very clearly a study of the effectiveness of Area Child Protection Committees in their own terms and in the terms set by the civil servants who provide them with guidance.

We began by introducing ourselves to each ACPC by writing to the chairperson explaining how we would be carrying out the research. At the same time we asked for certain written materials to be sent to us. These were: the local procedural handbook; the most recent annual reports; membership records of the ACPC; information on the financial operations of the ACPC; minutes of the ACPC for the past year. Later we asked for minutes of District Child Protection Committee meetings where these existed. The process of analysis of these documents is described later.

Interviews were then arranged with four members of each of the eight ACPCs. In order to give a clear focus to our work we decided to concentrate on representatives of what were clearly regarded as the most important agencies on the committees. We therefore arranged to see in each of the eight areas: a representative from social services (normally the child protection coordinator); a representative from the health service; a representative from the police; and a representative from the education service. This would enable us to look for consistencies and inconsistencies in views across the eight committees. At the same time we tried to give a relatively wide range of perspectives by selecting where we could from different roles within these principal agencies. For instance in one ACPC the person from the health service might be a consultant paediatrician, in another a senior nursing officer, in another a child psychiatrist. In addition, an interview was arranged with a representative from the NSPCC who as an individual sat on five different ACPCs and was therefore able to provide valuable comparative information.

Because of issues emerging in the first stage around the relatively autonomous roles of both general practitioners and headteachers, it was later agreed with the Welsh Office to extend the scale of project to enable us to undertake interviews with four headteacher and three general practitioner representatives. These were drawn from different ACPCs. The opportunity created by the extension was also used to interview a probation representative and a second NSPCC representative.

The interviews

The sample of those interviewed is described in Table 1.1

Table 1.1
Area Child Protection Committee representatives interviewed

Representative	A	B	C	D	E	F	G	H
Social Services - Coordinator	M	F	M	M		F	M	M
Social Services - Managers					F			
Health - Nursing		F				F		
Health - Child Psychiatrist				M				
Health - Paediatrician			M		M		M	F
Health - General Practitioners	M			M			M	
Education - LEA	F				M	M	F	M
Education - Headteacher	M		M	M				M
Police - Senior Police Rep	M	/	/	/	M	M	M	
Police - Family Support Unit	M	M		M				F
Probation					M			/
Others	/	/	/	/	/	F	/	F
Males	5	1	3	5	4	2	4	3
Females	1	2			1	3	1	3
Total	6	3	3	5	5	5	5	6
Representatives	7	5	5	7	6	5	6	7

(M = male; F = female)
N = 38

In a number of cases individuals sat on two or more Area Child Protection
Committees. This was useful for the Review, because these individuals were able to
compare processes across ACPCs. Most of them were interviewed in connection with
all their ACPC memberships. Where this is the case, the extra membership is

11

indicated by a slash (/), so that it does not count in terms of the numbers of people interviewed, but does count in terms of the number of 'representatives' interviewed.

The total number of individuals interviewed was 38, varying from three to six members of any one ACPC. The total number of members on Area Child Protection Committees in Wales at the time was approximately 171. The number interviewed therefore represents a sample of 22 per cent, or just over 1 in 5 of all ACPC representatives. Taking into account multiple representations this number rises to 48, representing a sample of 28 per cent or just over 1 in 4.

The total number of women we interviewed was 11 and the total number of men was 27, giving a ratio of male to female of 2.45 to 1. We did not actually have evidence of the gender balance of the committee membership overall; but since gender formed no part of the selection criteria for interview and our sample size was fairly large in proportion to the entire membership of the eight ACPCs, we believe that this closely reflects the actual overall gender balance of ACPCs.

All the interviews were carried out by the authors during the first three months of 1994 and were tape-recorded to ensure accuracy of recall, with the exception of three where the respondent refused consent. In general people had no objection to being tape-recorded although in a very few instances, interviewees requested that the tape recorder be switched off for brief periods during the interview, whilst sensitive 'off the record' material was discussed. Following interviews, the tapes were transcribed and prepared for analysis under subject headings.

After some general questions we asked respondents about their understanding and their view of Welsh Office policy; about the representation of agencies, including their own, on their committee; about the conduct of meetings, their efficiency and effectiveness; about the impact of their work on practice; and about the effect of organisational change on their work. The full set of preliminary questions is included as Appendix A.

On the basis of themes emerging from these interviews as significant or problematic, a schedule was developed for our meetings with the chairpersons of the eight Area Child Protection Committees. The interviews with chairpersons also laid stress on aspects of the work where the chairperson might have a different and perhaps broader perspective than that of individual Committee members.

In addition, respondents were asked to complete two follow-up questionnaires to assist in the quantitative analysis of the data. These concerned their view of various interagency relationships, the working of the Area Child Protection Committee from the chairperson's perspective, and its relationship with the Welsh Office.

Analysis of written material

The background to the review, and to a large extent the questions which we asked of those interviewed, were constructed in our preliminary examination of policy documents produced by the Welsh Office and by the Department of Health. The data on the composition and functioning of the ACPCs which was gathered from these interviews were then complemented by an examination of membership lists, reports and accounts, subcommittee structures, minutes of meetings, and local procedures handbooks. The conclusions from this analysis are in general incorporated within the text which follows, except where they need to be described separately.

In view of the significant role of the handbooks in informing practitioners of local policy and procedure, and transmitting Welsh Office policy, it was decided to carry out a comprehensive content analysis of each handbook for comparative purposes and to find out:

> 1) The extent to which the material within the handbooks conformed to Welsh Office policy
> and
> 2) Whether the level of detail of guidance would be sufficient to guide practice.

A detailed account of this analysis is given in chapter 6.

Conclusions and recommendations of the Welsh Office Review

The review concluded that Area Child Protection Committees appeared in general to be doing an excellent job of carrying out the functions for which they were set up, often in the face of considerable problems. ACPC members, especially chairpersons and child protection coordinators, were well informed about government policy. Agencies, with some exceptions, appeared satisfied with their representation, and ACPCs seem to have achieved a good mix of members with managerial authority and those with a deeper specialist knowledge of child protection issues. There was general agreement that interagency relationships had improved greatly as a result of the work of the committees.

However, the review also found that ACPCs continued to focus largely on investigative work, despite an obvious desire on the part of many of those involved to widen the scope of child protection work. The absence of any clear policies for follow-up and treatment, and the division between child protection services and those more generally concerned with children's wellbeing needed, we thought, to be urgently addressed. Child protection was operating separately from the rest of children's services and in particular from family support. This finding was in accord with others (Audit Commission, 1994; Colton et al, 1993; Jones and Bilton, 1994). The final report suggested that the scope of interagency collaboration, for which ACPCs offer a successful model, should be extended to develop strategies for all children in need. Children's services plans could play the same part in this process as the procedural handbooks appeared to have done for ACPCs to date. Finally, the review suggested that there was as yet little attempt to engage the energies or motivation of extended families and communities in the interests of prevention; and that more creative ways should be found to build on the strengths of families if partnership in child protection was to become a reality.

The review found that ACPCs were variable in size and composition, but that this was not necessarily undesirable since it partly reflected different local conditions. The Committees generally functioned effectively, especially those which had well established District Child Protection Committees. Handbooks were closely based on official guidance, but variations in coverage were a matter for concern. Unclear funding arrangements were a definite source of problems and tensions. Access to a budget would enable ACPCs to take a more active approach to aspects of child protection which they recognised to be underdeveloped, such as prevention and treatment.

It is essential that child protection interventions should be properly monitored and evaluated. If they had budgets ACPCs could take on an important role in conducting follow up studies and commissioning policy-related research. The Looking After Children assessment scheme could make a useful contribution to this process since comparative data would be available from the growing number of local authorities that are using it. A number of innovative models which had proved successful in other contexts were proposed and discussed: community-based family centres can overcome the problem of stigma and reduce the isolation often associated with abuse. Family group conferences and parent mutual aid associations were other models which seemed to offer many potential benefits. ACPCs could set up projects or provide the means to evaluate existing ones in order to see how they could best contribute to a more comprehensive and proactive child protection service.

The review concluded with a series of twenty recommendations in the following areas: child protection policy, reviews under Part 8 of *Working Together*, ACPC membership, committee structure, agency involvement, procedures handbooks, ACPC budgets, quality control, training, local government reorganisation and research.

Many of the conclusions of the review are developed further in this book, especially those which appear to have wider British or international application. Others, with more local or specific relevance, are given less emphasis.

Summary

Chapter 1 describes a study of the effectiveness of Area Child Protection Committees in Wales, from which much of the evidence in the book is derived and on which the argument is partly based. The study was commissioned by the Welsh Office and its emphasis reflects government concerns with the effectiveness of local services.

The terms of reference and methods of the Review are described, and its methodology briefly summarised. The study took the form of a series of interviews with members of ACPCs, supplemented by an examination of documentary material. The sample of representatives interviewed is described, and the way in which the interviews were conducted. The documentary analysis is also briefly described. The chapter ends with a summary of the conclusions and recommendations of the review.

2 Official policy and its interpretations

Although there has been considerable research over the past few years into the effectiveness of child care practice, there is relatively little evidence available on the effectiveness of policy work, particularly in the area of child protection policy. Policy directives come 'from the top', from central government, and by a number of routes are passed through local agencies to practitioners. There are numerous opportunities in the transmission process for policy to be modified before it gets to the practitioner level. On the other hand, there are various quality control measures in the transmission process to ensure policy is effectively transmitted. It is useful to have a definition of this effectiveness, and for the purposes of our research we used the following definition:

> The effective transmission of policy from Government, via local governmental agencies and interagency structures, to managers and practitioners.

This definition focuses on the process by which policy is relayed from one level to another, and the extent to which omissions, additions, amendments, interpretations and distortions take place in that process. There are also clearly opportunities for aspects of policy to be selected for particular emphasis, which in itself may sometimes constitute a type of distortion. Therefore we have tried to look at the comprehensiveness and the overall balance of policy; at whether all those features which seem to be important in the major government policy statements are reflected in the work of the Area Child Protection Committees, and at whether the relative emphasis given to different aspects of those policies centrally is maintained when they are 'operationalised' at the local level.

What is child protection policy?

One interpretation of child protection policy would include only those policies and services which are concerned with the identification of children who are being harmed or are likely to be harmed, and the action which may be taken to prevent further harm to those children. A broader view would see general preventative services including health, education, recreation, family support, and treatment services forming part of a comprehensive child protection policy.

A difficulty here is that whilst Government child protection policy in the past has encompassed a broad definition of child protection - for instance as in the description of the role of Area Child Protection Committees in paragraph 2.12 of *Working Together* (pp. 6-7), which is relatively broad in its scope - in terms of detailed guidance there has been a more limited view implied by government of the responsibilities of the committees. This has resulted in an assumption by many professionals that the narrower definition of child protection policy is the legitimate and officially-sanctioned view. This is an issue which we will need to discuss in more depth later, as it relates to one of the most important conclusions of our research.

What is government policy?

The expectation of the review was that it would take *official* child protection policy promulgated by the government as the starting point for an examination of the effectiveness of the work of the Area Child Protection Committees. This was clarified for us by the Welsh Office, and the following definition was used to indicate what should be included:

> All the guidance issued by or through the Welsh Office in the form of official publications, comprising *Working Together under the Children Act 1989, The Memorandum of Good Practice, The Guide for Undertaking a Comprehensive Assessment*, together with all relevant circulars issued by the Welsh Office to agencies (Jackson et al., 1994, p. 29)

The most important Welsh Office Circulars for our present purposes, including three issued after the Review was completed, are:

> WOC 54/93 - Protection of Children: Disclosure of Criminal Background of those with access to children

> WOC 38/93 - Guidance on Permissible Forms of control in children's residential care

> WOC 64/94 - Protection of Children: Disclosure of Criminal Background to Voluntary Sector Organisations

> WOC 60/95 - Child Protection: Clarification of Arrangements between the NHS and Other Agencies

WOC 35/96 - Child Care Procedures and Practice in North Wales: Implementation of the Report of Ms Adrianne Jones

In Wales most government circulars other than Home Office ones come form the Welsh Office. Often they are similar or identical to those issued by the Department of Health, the Department for Education and other London-based departments of state. Sometimes they are different, reflecting particular circumstances in Wales, different political emphasis on the part of Welsh ministers, or a different pace of policy implementation. For instance local government reorganisation has been a completely different process in Wales from in England, and the circulars relating to the implementation of children's services planning have been very different in Wales (see chapters 7 and 9). However, many of the policy documents with which we are concerned here are little different in Wales and in England. For example, Welsh Office Circular WOC 54/93 concerning criminal records disclosure is also issued as Home Office Circular HOC 47/93, Department for Education Circular DFE 9/93 and Department of Health Circular LAC 93(17). Welsh Office Circular WOC 64/94 concerning criminal records disclosure to the voluntary sector is also issued as Home Office Circular HOC 42/94 and Department of Health Circular LAC (94)22.

On occasion these differences between Wales and England appear to cause some confusion. For example, an interviewee from the police service pointed out to us that the police work to Home Office guidance, as opposed to Welsh Office guidance. The Welsh Office has responsibilities that in England are carried by a number of separate departments. However, there is no Welsh Office counterpart to the Home Office, whose operations extend across both England and Wales.

Policies and procedures

Many of these documents are as much about procedures for implementing policies as they are about the policies themselves. This points to an area of confusion which we found from the outset of our research, and which has been noted by others as well. Many of our respondents were unclear in general terms about certain key aspects of government child protection policy,and about what actually constituted government policy on this issue. In particular we found a great deal of confusion about the distinction between policy and procedures. This was particularly striking among representatives of the health and education services, who often seemed to equate the local procedures handbook with child protection policy; but social services and police representatives also frequently failed to distinguish between policy and procedure. This is in accordance with the findings of Diana Robbins (1990), who when requesting child care policy documents from English authorities received a wide variety of material ranging from procedures to manifestos. 'Many authorities seemed themselves to be unclear about how precisely to distinguish between the types of documents they were working on' (p.6). Gibbons (1997) considering specifically child protection policy, whilst acknowledging a high degree of clarity of procedures, notes the lack of clarity of policy which she attributes to the absence of clearly defined objectives.

In broad terms the policy governing an area of service provision may be defined as the stated objectives of the service, its priorities and its standards. Procedures specify how the service is to be provided in individual cases and in particular who has responsibility and authority for what. Making the distinction between policies and procedures can in practice sometimes be difficult, especially for those who are further removed from the formulation of policies and procedures and closer to actual service provision. Nevertheless we think it is an important distinction, of which both managers and practitioners need to have a working understanding if they are to perform effectively as professionals and not as mere functionaries; above all because they must be able to recognise the circumstances where to follow procedures slavishly might undermine the objectives of policy, but also to ensure that those aspects of policy which are governed by procedures do not assume a disproportionate weight in actual service provision. It is our contention that this is precisely what has happened in child protection.

One area where this confusion has an impact is in understanding the necessity for different ACPCs to be engaged in similar work. Government policy documents provide a focus around which agencies can come together and work out local policies and procedures. However, once together, views on the policy and procedures begin to differ. One difference is about how variable those policies should be from one area to another. For some ACPC representatives it is difficult to see the need for locally-written procedures. As put by one ACPC member:

> Why are we all sitting around in all these different groups around the country talking about the same things?

This implies a view of policy implementation that sees it as an uncritical process of doing as one is told. From another point of view it could be of supreme importance that there should be 'different groups around the country talking about the same things'. However, there is a view that detailed guidance on how and when to intervene could, and should, be produced nationally. This opinion often comes from agencies who cover more than one area and who have clearly defined authority structures. The police, who frequently have Force areas that overlap different ACPCs, spend considerable effort trying to ensure that the local policy is consistent between the two or three ACPC areas that they cover. Not surprisingly, they may consider it a waste of resources to be involved in the same process in a number of different areas.

In addition to emphasising the kind of confusion that may exist between policies and procedures, this example also reflects a variation between ACPC members on the extent to which procedures should be prescriptive and authoritative. For some managers the very term 'procedures' appeared to suggest that no discretion is allowed whereas 'guidelines' appeared to allow for judgement and some degree of flexibility. Both terms were found to be in wide usage. It is interesting that some saw the government's guidance on what procedures should be followed (for instance in *Working Together*) as being prescriptive, and agreed that this should be so. Others also saw the guidance as prescriptive but felt that it should be less so. Others in contrast thought that the guidance was fairly non-prescriptive and felt that it should be more prescriptive and allow less room for discretion. This range of views, both on how things are and how they should be, appeared to make for some challenging attempts to achieve consensus in decisions about child protection services.

Relationship between Area Child Protection Committees and central government

The relationship between local agencies and the government is clearly a significant factor influencing the mediation of child protection policy. In Wales at the time our research was carried out there were only eight Welsh social services authorities, and correspondingly only eight Area Child Protection Committees, relating to one central government department. This compared dramatically with the large number of local authorities in England relating to the Department of Health; a relationship which of necessity is often mediated through regional offices. Potentially therefore the Welsh Office is able to enjoy a much closer relationship with the local Area Child Protection Committees, with far more direct and intimate contact; although in practice we found that the extent of this appeared to vary considerably between counties. How this will develop now that the eight counties have been disaggregated into 22 unitary authorities remains to be seen.

Even with only eight counties wide variations were to be found in the nature of the relationship of ACPCs to the Welsh Office. Some idea of the range is given by the following comments from those we interviewed when we asked about their expectations and their experiences of the Welsh Office:

> 'Available, accessible, useful'
> 'It's getting better. I think it could be better still'

and on the other hand:

> 'I've no expectations of the Welsh Office'

Of course relationships, especially within Wales (where there is considerable contact), are both formal and informal. In general most people in Wales consider the informal relations to be much more satisfying than the formal relationships.

Factors that account for variations in the nature of the relationships between ACPCs and government may include: differences in political context; tensions that arise in the conduct of reviews and inspections; and the relative ability of government to help resolve local difficulties.

Differences in political context may lead to differences in emphases on how children can be most effectively protected from abuse. Child abuse is a political issue, and to some extent at least, one on which the politicians may be divided. This is particularly so where issues of resources are concerned; not only the resources available to provide social workers and other professionals with the means to deal with abuse once it has happened, but also the links between poverty and abuse. The multi-causal nature of child abuse which is now generally accepted, places an emphasis on causative factors that lie not only within individuals, families and their immediate environments, but also on factors within the community and societal contexts as well. The connection between social/economic deprivation and child abuse has been repeatedly demonstrated. Writers have noted the links between sexual abuse and the role of men within society. The connections between the acceptability of corporal punishment within society (which has been publicly endorsed on radio by a government minister) and the physical abuse of children, whilst not strongly tested empirically seems to many to be conspicuously obvious. All these matters may be the occasion for sharp political differences over what child abuse is and how best to overcome or respond to it.

Tensions that arise in the conduct of reviews and inspections (for example around deadlines and timetables for Part 8 reviews   - see chapter 8) may affect the relationship between the government officials and local agencies. For social services departments, inspections as a means of ensuring local adherence to national guidelines were implemented when the Social Service Inspectorate was set up in 1985, and since that time over 40 inspections of local authority child protection services have taken place (Social Services Inspectorate/Department of Health, 1993). Inspections will be considered more fully in chapter 3. Part 8 Reviews, which apply to Area Child Protection Committees corporately and not just to the social services department, are a more recent development since October 1991. Paragraph 8.1 of *Working Together* prescribes that such a review should be undertaken whenever a case '... involves an incident leading to the death of a child where child abuse is confirmed or suspected, or a child protection issue likely to be of major public concern'. Although coming into effect with the Children Act 1989, there were precursors to the part 8 reviews in part 9 of the previous edition of *Working Together* (Department of Health and Social Security/Welsh Office, 1988). Both inspections and reviews can put a strain on the relationships between social services departments or Area Child Protection Committees and the various central government agencies.

Part 8 Reviews are required to be submitted to the Department of Health via the local SSI region or to the Welsh Office. There are clearly specified timetable arrangements (paragraph 8.17), and it may be a source of some contention with ACPCs that the timetables often seem quite unrealistic. It is noteworthy that very few reviews are in fact completed within the specified time periods. In addition there is no explicit requirement for feedback from the Department of Health or the Welsh Office to local agencies, and in general there is a lack of clarity about the use to which Part 8 Reviews will be put, which creates additional tension.

The relative inability of government to help resolve local difficulties, or at least the local perceptions of that inability, may significantly affect local relationships with central government. In particular, negative feelings and perceptions may arise from the fact that ACPCs often find themselves trying to resolve at local level issues that are essentially national in character. What ACPC has not grappled with the vexed question of how to ensure that general practitioners take a more active part in child protection - both at ACPC level and in individual cases (see Simpson et al, 1994)?

Colton, Roberts and Sanders (1996) in their study of Part 8 reviews emphasised the need for GPs to be more involved in the child protection process. The NSPCC inquiry into prevention (Lord Williams of Mostyn, 1996) acknowledged the difficulty of involving general lpractitioners. Another example would be developing policy with the education service and others on the question of abuse by professionals. This is often a thorny issue, and one which has in itself been the focus of several Part 8 reviews as it gives rise to cause for public concern. These are not local issues, but they become local problems.

When local agencies are attempting to tackle problems that actually need to be sorted out at a national level, frustration and irritation with central government is likely to result. This is especially so if government is seen as demanding more effective interagency coordination at an operational level when what is sometimes needed, as one of our respondents put it, is 'better interagency coordination at policy level.'

Should the government give a clearer lead?

One view which was frequently expressed to us was that central government ought to be more proactive in policy development. There is according to one ACPC member, 'a sad lack of contact over policy issues in child protection on a regular basis'. The history of child abuse is of a continually changing arena into which new issues are emerging. Further research following the discovery of the battered baby syndrome led to the understanding that physical abuse is not limited to babies, and the coining of the term 'child abuse'. Child abuse later came to be understood as not only including physical abuse and neglect, but encompassing damage to the child's emotional and psychological growth as well under the heading 'emotional abuse'. In the late 70's and 80's it became known that many children were being used sexually by adults in ways which were now defined as abusive. In recent years further new issues in the field of child protection have emerged, requiring new policies and procedures, such as female genital mutilation, Munchausen's Syndrome by proxy, organised, ritual and satanic abuse, abuse by professionals such as foster carers or teachers, and abuse in residential schools and child care establishments.

The field was described by one ACPC chair as a 'moving stage'. Some practitioners and managers keep up to date by reading specialist journals, through membership of professional associations such as BASPCAN (the British Association for the Study and Prevention of Child Abuse and Neglect) or NOTA (the National Association for the Development of Work with Sex Offenders), and by attendance at conferences, a wide range of which are organised every year by a variety of organisations and agencies. However, in such a volatile situation it is not realistic to expect practice to wait upon the development of new guidance in the form of published documents like *Working Together*, even though they appear fairly regularly (two in the last eight years, and another revision to incorporate the 'refocusing debate' is expected). An ongoing dialogue, outside the formal context of inspections and Part 8 reviews, would create opportunities for local practice to reflect the latest thinking of central government, and would enable local practice to be informed by up-to-date knowledge.

In cases where the Welsh Office had been seen to give a clear lead, for example in relation to organised abuse, this generally seemed to have been welcomed by Area Child Protection Committees. Agencies would have welcomed just as eagerly further advice from government on the issue of abuse by professionals, which has caused considerable difficulties and strains within ACPCs. This is not to say that a closer, ongoing, involvement with government would be welcomed by all members of ACPCs. For some ACPC members there is a feeling of being quite distant from government, apart from the straightforward question of adhering to official guidelines. For some members child protection is essentially a local issue. For some ACPCs, the relationship with government is tense for a variety of reasons, not least of which is the different political contexts within which they operate. Thus any change in the level of activity on the part of government, however helpful in intent, may face the difficulty of meeting conflicting expectations.

Just as agencies had to overcome professional misgivings, different public accountabilities, and different professional understandings to be able to communicate more openly about how best to protect children, so similar barriers may sometimes have to be crossed in order to achieve better working relationships with government and its officials. The following extract from the second of the two studies of inquiry reports is relevant:

> One way of increasing effectiveness will be to improve contact between ACPCs, working in isolation and unco-ordinated... Such contact for policy development and role development is essential... There is a need too for ACPCs to feel a closer relationship to central Government from whom they clearly look for leadership. A working relationship between central Government and these committees is necessary to enable review and development of function. It is not clear that presently established links are sufficient to do this (Department of Health, 1991b, p. 54)

It is clear that the benefits of working together could be extended to include more than just the interagency protection of children, and the interagency management of child protection within a geographical area. It could incorporate a more proactive approach to developing ongoing dialogue between central and local agencies concerned with the protection of children. It could also include a more constructive dialogue between those governmental agencies responsible for child protection policy at the highest levels.

Summary

Chapter 2 began with a consideration of the basic terms used in managing child protection services. Working definition of 'effectiveness' and of 'government child protection policy' were adopted. Some of the difficulties in identifying the scope of child protection policy, and in distinguishing policy from procedures, were considered. Finally the relationship between Area Child Protection Committees and central government was examined. It was suggested that three factors could influence the nature of this relationship. These are differences in the political context, tensions that arise in the conduct of reviews and inspections, and the relative ability of government to help resolve local difficulties. The chapter concluded with a consideration of the advantages and disadvantages of government giving a clearer lead on child protection issues than it already does.

3   Putting policy into practice

A key task of an Area Child Protection Committee is to see that government policy is transmitted to practitioners in such a way that they are able to implement it effectively. This is not a trivial point; in fact the effectiveness of this process may be said to be at the heart of the British approach to child protection. The system's emphasis on structured investigation, on formal procedures, and on relatively rigorous interagency coordination, together with the regular review of policy and procedures from the top, demand the existence of reliable mechanisms for ensuring that a clear and accurate understanding of current policy informs the actions of practitioners when they are engaged in work on individual cases. To some extent these mechanisms are offered by the relationships between central government and individual agencies. To a very great extent, however, they depend on the working of Area Child Protection Committees.

These mechanisms have not always been seen to work well. One of the themes which accompanied the introduction of the Children Act was the failure of earlier policy changes to have sufficient impact on practice, and this was one of the reasons for the unprecedented investment in training and preparation for implementation in the period after that Act received the Royal Assent. (See Masson, 1994.) Concern by government about the occasional disappearance of good intentions is expressed in 'Where did the guidance go', an exercise included in the Department of Health publication *Patterns and Outcomes in Child Placement* (Department of Health, 1991c). This invites the reader to consider a hypothetical scenario in which a child has died as a result of abuse and in which there are indications that local procedures had not been followed. The intention is to encourage practitioners and managers to enquire within their own agencies about the mechanisms whereby practitioners are kept informed of the procedures which they are supposed to be operating.

There are a great many policies and procedures which emanate from central government and which have implications for agencies providing child protection services. These include not only initiatives such as *Working Together* but also the circulars referred to earlier which are issued from time to time on specific matters or aspects of agency working. Action has to be taken on each occasion to ensure that the messages contained in these instruments reach the staff whose work they are intended to affect. Sometimes this is quite specific; for instance, the circular WOC 60/95 (Child Protection: Clarification of Arrangements between the NHS and Other Agencies) explicitly required that ACPCs review their policies and procedures concerning accountabilities of health representatives and that District Health Authorities, NHS Trusts and Family Health Service Authorities distribute copies to relevant named postholders; for example, copies were to be provided to each designated doctor and designated nurse.

On other occasions the spread of relevance may be less obvious and agencies or ACPCs must consider how best to disseminate the new information. For example, a document as significant as WOC 54/93 (Protection of Children: Disclosure of Criminal Background of those with access to children) has wide ranging implications for procedures to be adopted when engaging staff, volunteers, students, etc. by a wide range of organisations. Likewise, Welsh Office Circular WOC 35/96 (Child Care Procedures and Practice in North Wales: Implementation of the Report of Ms Adrianne Jones), has implications for service operation well beyond the direct relevance for protecting children in residential care. All of these have relevance for the agencies attempts to ensure that the daily work of practitioners operates within the policy and procedures context established by central government.

In the previous chapter we were at pains to emphasise the difference between policies and procedures. In this one we will frequently need to talk of both in the same breath, because our concern is with the ways in which both are communicated to practitioners, and in the process the distinction between the two may often be blurred. Much of what emanates from the centre includes a mixture of explicit policy statement, implicit policy, and procedural guidance or prescription. When policy is interpreted and 'operationalised' locally it often is translated into procedural terms, both in the writing and rewriting of interagency guidance and through managerial directives and instructions. It is these processes which we will now discuss.

How is policy made known at operational level?

In chapter 2 we looked at how government policies are understood by those who represent their agencies on the Area Child Protection Committees, and at some of the factors that appear to influence that understanding. We now want to look at the processes whereby those policies are communicated to staff in the field. It appears that this is in large measure a process that occurs within the constituent agencies of the ACPC, although in some areas the district child protection committees (see below) may have an important part to play as well.

When new policies or procedures are promulgated, Area Child Protection Committees have to consider the implications of those policies or procedures for their local areas. Very often the detailed consideration takes place in a 'Policy and Procedures' subgroup, which may either be a standing committee or an ad hoc body set up for the occasion. The result of this consideration is likely to be an amendment to the agreed interagency policies and procedures. Once this has been agreed, it then becomes the responsibility of the constituent ACPC agencies to implement it using their own intra-agency processes. Although there may be joint training in order to help develop a stronger collaborative element to the way in which practitioners from different agencies operate the new policy, the primary responsibility for seeing that all relevant staff have an adequate understanding of the policy, and that they can be relied upon to follow it, usually rests firmly with the individual agencies.

However, those individual agencies often have very different internal managerial relationships, and as a result the processes whereby policies and procedures are transmitted may vary considerably. For some, even the notion of 'staff' within an 'agency' appears somewhat inappropriate. This is most obviously the case with general practitioners; although they are considered below as a special case, much of the following discussion is less relevant to them as a group than to others. The same applies to a lesser extent to headteachers, who are also relatively autonomous in relation to the local education authority structures.

There are a number of mechanisms through which locally agreed policy can be transformed into practice. These include internal management systems, written guidelines and procedures, training, and delegate feedback arrangements.

By 'internal management systems' here we mean the intra-agency arrangements for directing practice in individual cases. They usually include some form of senior managerial forum, of which ACPC representatives will often be members by virtue of their managerial roles within the agency. Such systems also include structures which allow for policy and procedures to be transmitted to the geographical subdivisions of the agency, and from there to practitioners within the subdivision. There may be a varying number of layers or strata in these systems, with different levels of strategic responsibility. Billis, Bromley, Hey and Rowbottom (1980) provide a model of such systems for social services departments. However they are structured in detail, one characteristic which these groupings have in common both within and between agencies is that they all receive policy and procedural directives from the levels above them as input, and pass on similar directives as output to the levels below them. This 'chain of command' approach has been described by Weber as a feature of bureaucracies.

All agencies will have some form of written instructions setting out for staff how they should undertake their responsibilities. At the very least these are likely to include person and job specifications developed at the time when a post is created and filled. However, in addition agencies may also have internal procedures manuals, standing orders, and other forms of internal circular. Where these are produced they are usually sufficiently detailed to guide practice, and will indicate the correct way to intervene in a variety of situations which a practitioner may be expected to encounter on a regular basis. However, it is not always the case that every member of staff has their own copy of all this guidance. The costs of production and distribution have to be found from limited budgets and it may be, for instance, that only first-line managers have complete copies of guidelines and procedures. Sometimes distinctions are made between information that all practitioners need to know as a generic baseline, and information that is only essential to specialists in the particular field of child protection. Some agencies may not have their own internal guidance in relation to child protection, but may instead rely exclusively on the interagency local procedures handbook produced by the ACPC.

Written internal guidance or procedures are closely linked to the internal management system. A senior member of staff is likely to have had responsibility for the drafting of the procedures and guidelines. Even if they are not actually produced by members of the agency's management team, they will almost certainly have to be approved by that team. Further, it is through the management structure of the agency that they are passed on to the operational staff who will need to put them into effect, whether those be designated teachers, social work team leaders, senior nursing staff, or whoever. The same personnel and systems are of course responsible for the transmission of interagency policies and procedures.

Training is another vital means of ensuring that government policy is passed on to practitioners. Virtually all the professions represented on ACPCs have arrangements for ongoing training and development. For teachers the provision of ongoing training is supplied through INSET days, which are limited to two per term. But there are prioritisation and funding difficulties when consideration is given to the use of these for child protection training to teachers (to be discussed below). Police have their own training programmes which as a minimum are likely to include familiarity with Force requirements concerning how to respond to child abuse incidents. General practitioners have a requirement to undertake minimum amounts of training as part of their continuing medical education (although ACPCs have not yet quite worked out how this might be used to promote awareness of child protection issues for this group).

By and large however, the major providers of child protection training are the social services departments. These departments have training sections within which child protection training has greatly developed through the provision of the government funded Training Support Programme. In addition to the separately provided in-house training, interagency training - which is usually coordinated by social services - has provided opportunities for staff from different agencies to train together. Often the presence of an ACPC training subcommittee will facilitate the arrangements for the provision of interagency training.

Until recently there was a dramatic expansion and proliferation of social services department trainers specialising in children and families (and latterly in child protection) between 1989 (the time of the introduction of the Training Support Programme) and 1995. Previously departments might have had only one trainer addressing the training needs of all the various client interest groups within social services. Subsequently there emerged specialist forums for child protection trainers to gather and consider common issues and dilemmas facing them. However, the reorganisation of local government, in Wales at least, reversed this trend. Because of the limitations of smaller administrative units, and because of sharply reduced budgets, many trainers have had to revert to being more generic instead of specialising in a particular area..

One further way in which agencies achieve the dissemination of government policy is by the use of ACPC delegate feedback arrangements. This is especially relevant for those representatives who come from agencies with a less tightly defined managerial structure, and who may represent a relatively large group of peers; it applies particularly therefore to general practitioners and headmasters. In some cases there are arrangements for a representative to be appointed on behalf of the group and for them to provide regular feedback to that group. This may be through a formal nomination and election process, or may be more informal. To the extent that this is the system, a

27

greater proportion of the child protection information may reach practitioners directly from their representative on the Area Child Protection Committee, rather than through the bureaucratic structure of their agency.

This last point suggests that there may be more general differences between the constituent agencies in the strategies they adopt for passing on government policy to their personnel. Simply because of the differences in their functions, the means of policy dissemination within agencies is likely to be different. We have therefore looked at how these four methods of policy dissemination are used by the main participants in the child protection process. In the next section we will report on what we found.

Social services

Social services tend to rely on the first three methods of distributing information about policy: internal management systems, written guidelines and training. Social services departments are very complex bureaucratic structures which have clear 'chain of command' accountabilities at the various levels within which they operate. The structures may vary depending upon the nature of the area being served and beliefs of those in post about the kinds of management structure required to meet the needs of the local community In the mid 1970s there were no specialist child protection teams, and few if any child protection workers. Child protection work was undertaken within the context of the post-Seebohm genericism of social work.. The expansion of child protection work in the last twenty five years has meant that at the point of delivery services have become much more specialised, and this has of necessity been reflected within the managerial structures.

An important mechanism for the *internal management* of such a complex agency as social services is regular meetings of varying frequency. There are basically two types of meetings: those of individuals at the same managerial level and those of a manager and the individuals that he or she manages. In some cases there may be meetings across more than two managerial levels. Meetings with team leaders and meetings of principal officers who are responsible for the management of geographical regions are typical methods of ensuring that policy and procedures are transmitted to practitioners. Reorganisations of the managerial structures may sometimes be necessary to clarify managerial accountabilities and to fill perceived gaps in the managerial system. Indeed, despite its many difficulties, one positive benefit of local government reorganisation in Wales has been that it has allowed managers to correct anomalies in their systems that had been previously identified but which perhaps would not have been addressed if the system had not undergone the dramatic change of complete reorganisation.

The extent of reliance on *internal written guidelines* (for example a 'procedures manual' or the equivalent) is variable between social services departments. It is easy for a practitioner operating in a department which has a comprehensive, regularly updated manual to assume that this is how operations at the point of delivery are directed in all agencies. This would be a false assumption.

Where there are procedures manuals for social services staff, then there is the need for these to be in harmony with the interagency child protection procedures developed by the Area Child Protection Committee discussed more fully in chapter 6. There are two reasons for the use of intra-agency procedures in addition to the agreed interagency ones. The first is to supplement the interagency handbook with greater operational detail, perhaps reflecting the detail of the agency structure as it changes from time to time or perhaps reflecting the relationship between child protection activity and other departmental services. The other is to respond to urgent need. The production of written interagency policy and procedures can be slow to be developed within ACPCs (which tend to meet around four times per year, sometimes six, and very rarely more frequently). In response to this delay, social services departments frequently issue their own internal procedural circulars in advance of ACPC policy and procedures being produced (for example on the basis of a Welsh Office circular). As one respondent said:

> We try to operate it on an informal level to start with. We wouldn't wait for ACPC to put it in tablets of stone

Child Protection Coordinators based in social services departments are very much involved in the development of the ACPC's interagency procedures for child protection, often through their role in a local Policy and Procedures sub-group. Although Child Protection Coordinators may see themselves as primarily agents of the Area Child Protection Committee, with multi-agency responsibilities, they are also likely to have the additional responsibility for drafting any internal procedures that may be required for social services.

However, local internal procedures do not always exist apart from the child protection local procedures handbook. In at least two of the Welsh social services departments this lack of an internal practice guide was explicitly identified as a deficiency, and there were indications that the same might apply to other areas. Problems arise especially where interagency procedures are lacking in sufficient detail to guide practice. Where internal procedures do exist, the best of these will have senior managers specifically responsible for their development, distribution, and revision. They will be sufficiently comprehensive and jargon-free for practitioners to find them of positive assistance in carrying out their day to day functions.

The connection between *training* for social services staff and child protection policy can, and in many cases is, assured through the child protection trainer being a member of the Area Child Protection Committee (although this is not an explicit requirement in appendix 5 of *Working Together*). Like the role of the child protection coordinator, the role of the child protection trainer may be seen as more than simply that implied by the social services interest, as ACPCs concern themselves with the provision of interagency training as well as training for social workers. Hitherto this interagency training has been largely dominated by joint training in investigation for police and social workers in accordance with the emphasis provided in paragraph 7.2 of *Working Together*. So far there are limited signs of its extension to joint training with other professionals or to the non-investigatory aspects of child protection.

Training is also used as a way of informing staff of new procedures or changes in the child protection system. In fact it could be argued that training, which is more widespread even than the provision of internal procedures manuals, is the most important means by which social services staff are made aware of what is required of them in child protection.

The health service

The modern health service has a far more complex management structure than the other principal agencies involved in child protection. It is dominated by powerful professions which to a greater or lesser extent have their own chain of command. In recent years additional elements of generic management have been introduced, and at the same time the service has been broken up organisationally into a variety of units of different size with responsibility either for commissioning or for providing services. This creates a problem for the efficient dissemination of policies and procedures to operational staff (and their immediate managers where they have them). In response to this one official approach has been to give certain key professionals some of the responsibility for this work. In *Working Together* (Appendix 9: p. 120-121) there are described three health-related roles, the designated senior doctor, the designated senior nurse and the designated senior midwife, all of which carry the personal responsibility for ensuring that effective communication systems exist in relation to child protection.

The role of the designated doctor is to advise on the content of contracts in relation to child protection so that commissioning agents can ensure that in all health providing services concerned with children the following apply:

i) Child protection policies are in agreement with ACPC policy;

ii) Effective communication systems exist to coordinate work between different provider units (hospital, community child health service, school health service) including an efficient systems for transferring records;

iii) A source of information and advice on child protection is available to all doctors and other health professionals who come into contact with children;

iv) Doctors know how, and under what circumstances, to contact social services departments about the use of the child protection register.
(*Working Together*, p.120)

In addition:
Each provider unit concerned with children should have, or be able to call on the services of, at least one senior doctor with a high level of skill and expertise in child protection ...
(*Working Together*, p.120)

30

The role of the designated senior nurse and the role of the designated senior midwife are described as:

- Ensuring that effective child protection policies are in place in all provider units, Directly Managed Units (DMUs) and NHS Trusts and they are in agreement with ACPC policy;

- Setting up an effective communication system to co-ordinate work between provider units, DMUs and NHS Trusts;

- Acting as a reference point for other agencies SSD, LEA, FHSA, Police, NSPCC, etc;

- Monitoring the system for transferring nursing and midwifery records within and between health authorities;

- Ensuring that provider units are aware of the names of the children in their care who are on the child protection register;

- Identifying training needs.

(Working Together, p.121)

The roles of senior nurses, health visitors, and midwives have been further clarified in guidance (Department of Health, 1992a) and are currently undergoing further development.

There are a wide range of representatives from the various health disciplines on Area Child Protection Committees. *Working Together* suggests five specific sources of representation: 1) district health authority management; 2) medical and psychiatric representatives, which would include paediatricians, child psychiatrists, and occasionally adult psychiatrists; 3) nursing representative which would include both health visiting and midwifery services in the community as well as hospital nursing; 4) family health services authority (FHSA) management; 5) a general practitioner representative of the local medical committee.

Like their colleagues in social services departments, health professionals (apart from general practitioners treated separately below) also tend to rely on the first three methods of disseminating information about policies; internal management systems, written guidelines or procedures, and training. However, there are some unique difficulties to be addressed because of the diverse and even fragmented character of agencies within the health service. As we suggested above, even before the health reforms there were divisions in the health service which could affect the provision of child protection services, that were not present to the same extent in other agencies. Cutting across the divisions between community based health services and hospital based health services are the divisions between medical and nursing services, as shown in the table 3.1 below:

31

Table 3.1
Health service divisions

	Community Health Services	Hospital Services
Medical	Child Psychiatrists	Child Psychiatrists
	Community Paediatricians	Hospital Paediatricians
	General Practitioners	
Nursing	Health Visitors	Paediatric Nurses
	Midwives	

Like social services, health service providers have a clear *line management structure*, but with services relevant to child protection being provided by diverse sectors within the services. Units that are more spread out, such as those providing community services, tend to use meetings and the line management structure for communicating policy. In the Welsh Office Review, some respondents identified differences in patterns between community health services and hospital services, indicating a more structured approach within the community health services, and difficulty in getting information into the hospital systems. Hospital workers did not have the same level of input into child protection matters as community health workers for instance. Child protection was seen as 'not their problem'. A different ethos towards child protection within hospitals was also seen as the source of some of the difficulties which arose; for example health visitors were not always informed of children who attended at casualty departments. From the point of view of managing child protection services and disseminating policy and procedures, there were seen to be clear advantages where children's health services were unified across community and hospital settings.

Recent reports have looked in detail at nursing in relation to child protection, and one of the findings was that the role of the designated nursing officer as defined in *Working Together* varied from area to area. In some areas, the role is very much as indicated in *Working Together*. It is concerned with managerial functions such as policy dissemination, communication and monitoring. In others, however, it is described as being much more in line with that of a clinical nurse specialist (child protection); that is '... attending case conferences, assisting with preparation of court statements, attendance at court, training and day to day management of child protection issues' (CANO, 1993, 4th draft). The report goes on to point out that 'this does not allow for the strategic overview of services that is essential'. The same point is made in the recent report by the Royal College of Nursing (RCN), *Nursing and Child Protection*, (RCN, 1994), which goes on to make other points about the additional, non child protection, responsibilities carried by designated nurses.

In relation to the use of *written material* in the health service, we found that the main method for ensuring that staff had written information on policy and procedures was the availability of both *Working Together* and the local procedures handbook. In general the availability was considered by those we interviewed to be adequate.

Nursing representatives also referred to 'nursing procedures' and internal guidelines circulated to senior nursing staff for transmission to field staff. In one area minor administrative difficulties in distributing copies of the local procedures handbooks had caused delay in distribution, but had also had the benefit of subjecting the methods of distribution of material in general within the Health service to scrutiny and subsequent modification.

Within health service agencies, *training* is a vital means of ensuring adherence to policy. The provision of regular training to staff, both on basic courses, and on multi-agency courses is considered by health senior staff to be an important means of keeping operational health staff informed of policy and procedures within child protection. Senior staff who are involved in the systems for managing child protection internally, are likely to be involved directly in the provision of training to staff.

General Practitioners

It is noticeable how often general practitioners describe themselves, and are described by others, as 'self-employed'. This is clearly a status which is perceived to create difficulties for the interagency management of child protection. The use of the term by respondents often seemed to imply a lack of accountability, at least within the system responsible for the management of child protection.

The nature of the relationship between GPs and the family health service authorities (FHSAs), mediated to some extent by the local medical committees (LMCs) is clearly different from the relationship of other professionals to their agencies. As Bury and Elston (1987) put it: ' ...general practitioners and hospital doctors operate separately, both from each other and from the social services'.

The expectation, taken for granted in most child protection agencies, that staff receive instructions about policy and procedures from an employer who can compel performance, does not apply in the same way to the general practitioner service. General practitioners are conscious that their status is in this respect different from that of other representatives. One GP in the Welsh Office Review put it particularly clearly:

> Everybody else there [on ACPC] is representing an agency of some sort and has a management structure, which can be used to cascade information down. In general practice it's much more difficult in that general practitioners are independent contractors, self employed who contract into the health service. There isn't a structure either for them to instruct me as to what I should be saying, nor for me to cascade down information.

As GPs are in this way *sui generis* - although there are, as we shall see, some similarities with the position of headteachers - it is important that child protection systems should be flexible enough to adapt to take advantage of their contribution. With a great deal of goodwill and motivation, some local systems seem able to achieve a relatively high degree of participation and enthusiasm from general practitioners fairly successfully; most, however, have difficulty.

As one might expect, *delegate feedback arrangements* assume a greater importance in communicating policy to general practitioners than in relation to other roles represented on the ACPC. Because of the nature of GPs' contractual position, the distinction between delegate feedback arrangements and *internal management systems* is not absolutely clear-cut. Policy developed at the Area Child Protection Committee is communicated to other general practitioners via the mechanisms through which GP representatives have come to sit on the ACPC. This will in general involve feeding back to the local medical committee (LMC), the local elected body of GP representatives. However, despite the explicit reference in *Working Together* to GP representatives being members of the local medical committee, it is not always the case that they are. Representatives may also use the services of the Family Health Services Authority to disseminate information. The LMC negotiates with the FHSA (and it also passes concerns and information up to the general practitioners' national negotiating body, the General Medical Council).

The ability of the general practitioner representative to communicate to colleagues may be limited because it is very likely that there will be no formal means of communication established in a locality for general practitioners to communicate with each other. There may be no vehicles other than the written information disseminated through the FHSA for ideas to be shared in a two way dialogue. One GP representative whom we interviewed suggested that the information from ACPCs about child protection policy and procedures would be more likely to reach GPs directly from the ACPC rather than through non-existent or limited GP communication networks. As this respondent saw it, the role of the GP on the ACPC is more to ensure that the ACPC does not undertake policy and procedural decisions which may be against the interests of general practitioners, than to facilitate the means by which the child protection work of general practitioners may be in accord with locally agreed policy and procedures. To that extent the process of representation for this group is one-way.

The distribution of *written information* to GPs is generally the function of the FHSA. (In fact the role of the FHSA in the management of child protection would appear to be largely limited to this role.) In general GPs will have their own personal copy of the local procedures handbook, and this should be available to other members of the primary health care team. However, in some cases the distribution of the handbook may be problematic because of disputes over whose financial responsibility it is. Apart from the handbook, the main source of written information is the material (which may be in the form of a newsletter) distributed by the FHSA to all general practitioners within their area. Child protection information for the FHSA to distribute may come from the GP representative, or it may come direct from the ACPC.

Considering the extent to which other agencies use *training* as a means of disseminating policy, it is remarkable how little it features in respect of GPs. It seems that it may be potentially useful to overcome some of the difficulties that have been found in ensuring that policies and procedures are well understood among this group of professionals. Child protection material could be included in courses on child health surveillance, and courses aimed at trainee general practitioners, as well as continuing education for those in practice. It is surprising how little use is made of the role of the CME (continuing medical education) tutor to promote training for general practitioners in child protection. The CME tutor has the responsibility for organising postgraduate education for GPs. There are requirements for GPs to have a modest amount of continuing education, through attendance at approved courses. Course approval is undertaken by CME tutors, based on the educational content. At present, most CME tutors are probably unaware of the importance and relevance of child protection training. Closer liaison between the CME tutor and the ACPC (perhaps with the chair of the Training Subcommittee where it exists, or with the social services child protection trainer) could be helpful in this regard.

The police

As we observed earlier, the police tend to have a strong interest in the consistency of policy and procedures across the various ACPCs areas that each Force typically covers. In addition, the police have to distinguish between what every officer needs to know and what those who are more involved in child protection, such as family support unit (FSU) officers will need to be familiar with. This distinction is not unique to the police; however, it is particularly striking in an agency where any operational officer is likely to be involved in child protection from time to time (and has a personal statutory responsibility in this respect) but where a small group of staff are dealing with it virtually on a full-time basis and have a key responsibility for managing the investigative process. (Family Support Units are not uniformly available across the country, but where they do exist, they seem to be highly regarded. They may have slightly differing functions depending upon the Force they operate under. In some areas they are involved with rape and domestic violence, while in others they specialise solely in child abuse matters.)

In transmitting policy and procedures the police seem to place less emphasis on *management systems* than on the use of written material and on training. Whilst senior level management meetings are used for the consideration and determination of policy, a managerial structure is not used as much for its transmission. This is not to say that the 'chain of command' is not important; in some ways it is more so than in any other agency. Questions about authority levels are more clearly understood within the police service than within other agencies. Police representatives on ACPCs, we found, are likely to be very clear on the possibilities and limitations on their contributions to ACPC decisions.

To a greater extent than the other agencies, the bulk of the work of the police is governed by *written procedures* and detailed specifications, many of which have a legislative basis, and which every officer needs to have at his or her fingertips. This perhaps fits well with a procedural approach to child protection. For police officers who undertake specialist work in child protection, a copy of the local procedures handbook and *Working Together* are likely to be made available, usually at the time of the original specialist child protection training. For the rest of the Force, information about what beat officers need to know about child protection is contained in detailed written instructions which inform officers how to intervene in a variety of situations. They were described to us as 'standing orders' or 'the guide'. The guidance provided on child protection is most likely to have been produced by the police ACPC representative and to include a precis of information derived from authoritative sources such as ACPC guidelines, *Working Together* and the Children Act 1989.

Police *training* in child protection appears to be largely directed at those undertaking child protection investigations. The provision of specialist training tends to be easier in those Forces where there are specialist units dealing with child protection matters; certainly where the police take part in interagency training the participants are usually from FSUs or their equivalent, although community police officers may also be involved in some local interagency training.

The education service

As with the health service, education authorities are also required to have specific individuals who are designated to take on child protection responsibility. This applies both within schools and within the administrative structures of the local education authority. All schools are required to have a 'designated teacher' (*Working Together*, p.120). This person should be a 'senior member of staff with specific responsibility for co-ordinating action within the school and for liaising with social services departments' over individual cases of abuse (actual or suspected). Their role is to ensure 'that locally established procedures are followed, and particularly to act as the channel for communicating to the social services department relevant concerns...' In primary schools the usual practice is for the individual designated to be the head teacher. In secondary schools it is likely to be a deputy headteacher, often one who has responsibility within the school for pastoral care.

Working Together also offers guidance on the role of the designated officer within the local education authority; he or she should have 'responsibility for co-ordinating education service - including youth service - policy and action on child protection' (*Working Together*, p.120). The same individual should also: ensure that local procedures are in place, including the arrangements for designated teachers; be the point of contact for other agencies on child protection matters; and should normally be the person who represents the LEA on the ACPC.

As a result of the education reforms in recent years, LEAs have become smaller as much of the funding of education has been devolved directly to schools. The relationship of LEAs to schools has changed, and the methods of disseminating information about child protection policy have had to change as well. Regardless of whether schools have sought grant-maintained status, with the introduction of LMS (local management of schools) and devolved budgets, all schools have become more independent from the local education authority than they were in the past. 'Schools are certainly acting autonomously', as one headteacher who spoke to us put it.

Education representatives tended to rely on *written material* and *training* to disseminate information, although training for education staff has become problematic. For both LEA and headteacher representatives, the effectiveness with which they are able to represent schools has to be questioned. For LEA representatives, there may be fairly formal methods for ensuring that the responsibility for awareness of child protection policy and procedures is taken on by the schools. For example, whilst in some areas there is a procedure whereby LEAs send out to every designated teacher a form to sign and return indicating that they both have a copy of the local procedures manual and that they acknowledge their child protection responsibilities, in others the process seems to be far more haphazard.

In relation to the *internal management system* within education, the first point that must be emphasised is that the connections between schools are variable and often tenuous. This means that for headteacher ACPC representatives it is difficult for them to feel that they are representing anything other than their own school. The headteacher representative is likely to have very little information about what goes on in other schools, and to have no sense of a mandate from other schools about how to represent them. Like general practitioners discussed previously, headteachers are speaking more from the viewpoint of a headteacher, rather than on behalf of headteachers.

In general there is no specific forum where designated teachers can meet to consider child protection issues. To that extent theirs seems to be an isolated role. They may try to use existing general forums such as regular meetings of headteachers to raise child protection issues, but child protection does not usually have a high profile on these occasions, and tends to be discussed rarely. Headteachers have described how their involvement with Area Child Protection Committees has increased their awareness to such an extent that they feel confident that child protection issues would be properly addressed in their own school. Unfortunately, however, they rarely if ever feel that their involvement is having any effect on how child protection matters are addressed in other schools in their ACPC area.

In the first place, headteacher representatives are not necessarily aware of how child protection is dealt with by other schools, and therefore have no way of knowing if there is any consistency in practice. For example, they are unlikely to know if there is any agreement between schools on the question of what types of concerns will be referred to the social services. We found this to be an area of particular concern in the Welsh Office Review. One respondent commented on the extreme variations in referral patterns between schools, and in one area the view was expressed that a majority of teachers would probably not know what to do if they were confronted with a child with suspicious bruising. These findings are also supported in the literature. Campbell and Wigglesworth (1993) survey the child protection training needs of teachers, and report that whilst teachers 'consider child protection to be an important subject of direct relevance to their work ... 40 per cent of teachers did not feel confident in handling these issues'. Nor does the particular difficulty about referrals from education seem limited to Britain. In one study it was found that teachers both failed to report and mishandled suspected cases of child abuse (Levin, 1983). Briggs and Hawkins (1997) describing the situation in Australia, list eight reasons why teachers might not report, including distrust of the community welfare agency, inadequate training of what to look for, and fear of repercussions from parents. Tite (1993) reports that in Ontario, teachers 'preferred informal intervention over formal reporting' and their reporting was complicated 'by the perception that some cases can be handled more effectively by the school, without the intervention of the Child

Protection Services'. This is not necessarily wrong, but it is not consistent with the approach to handling child protection usually adopted in both Britain and North America as it is usually understood in key agencies such as police and social services; and therefore to the extent that this perception in schools is held it is likely to lead to difficulty.

Among the local education authority representatives to whom we spoke, there was a frequently-expressed view that designated teachers are not able to fulfil their role to bring child protection policy into the schools in a consistent way. To the extent that this is done, it is likely to be attributable to the particular qualities of the individual occupying the role rather than to the system itself being an effective one.

In general LEA representatives and headteacher representatives appear to see the relationships between LEAs and schools as very positive. However, those relationships are generally built upon networks established at a time when the LEAs had clear responsibilities for all matters affecting schools in their areas. Whether they will continue in a period when those responsibilities are diminished remains to be seen. The informality of relationships with LEA officers, and their availability to offer advice not just to designated teachers but to any teacher with a problem, are seen to facilitate good working partnerships within the current framework of education services.

LEA representatives are normally responsible for circulating *written material* about child protection both to staff of the authority and to schools. It can be expected that the interagency child procedures handbook will be made available to every school within an ACPC area. In rare cases, decisions may be taken to circulate a copy to every teacher, although this is more likely to be the case either where there have been particular problems with education approaches to child protection or where there are clear distinctions between the type of written material produced for child protection specialists and material produced for the wider group of professionals who may have more infrequent contact with child abuse.

As described previously, it is not uncommon in the current climate of decentralised control of education services for LEA representatives to ensure that they have fulfilled their responsibilities under *Working Together* by requiring designated teachers to sign to indicate that they have an updated copy of the local procedures handbook and that they are aware of their responsibilities as a designated teacher seems to be a common practice. Whether this process has any real impact on increasing awareness of non-designated teachers and ultimately on protecting children would be difficult to establish. It may be more reflective of the 'cover your back' approach (Carson, 1996) which has come to be characteristic of much child protection work.

Training is predominantly aimed at designated teachers; other teachers get very little, if any, training in child protection. Even where training is provided free of charge through multi-agency training facilitated by social services, teachers are often unable to take up opportunities because of the very high cost of paying supply teachers to provide cover. These costs come out of tightly controlled locally managed school budgets. School governing bodies which manage these budgets are given virtually no training in their child protection responsibilities. Even those publications which have been written to assist governors in understanding their role (Mahoney, 1988; Sallis,

1988; Leonard, 1989; Baker, 1990) make no mention of child abuse or work with social services departments.

'Inset' days are not generally available for child protection training because they are taken up with the demands of National Curriculum training. From a teaching perspective, training in the national curriculum is obligatory; training in child abuse, even such important and fundamental areas as the recognition and identification of abuse, is optional. The absence of budgets for child protection within LEAs and the shortage of staff who are equipped to deliver child protection training from an education perspective are further difficulties.

Summary

Chapter 3 began with a consideration of how policy is made known at operational level. Four general methods are described: internal management systems, written guidelines and procedures, training, and delegate feedback arrangements. The approaches of the principal agencies - social services, health (with general practitioners considered separately), police and education - are then described, looking at the extent to which they rely on each of the four methods.

Social services tend to rely on the first three methods. Health agencies have specifically designated roles for the coordination of practice in child protection, and these are described. These roles have become even more important in the context of the changes in the organisation of the health service which have made communications more difficult because of the diversity of agencies involved. Within health agencies there is a reliance on the first three methods as well. General practitioners however are treated as a separate case within health services because of their unique level of autonomy. They tend to rely on delegate feedback arrangements, in conjunction with the Family Health Services Authority and the Local Medical Committee.

The police, often covering multiple ACPC areas, have a strong interest in the child protection policy and procedures being consistent across those different ACPCs. They tend to place more emphasis on written material and training for the communication of policy than on the use of management systems, although the management systems are particularly well defined (in terms of 'chain of command' and levels of responsibility).

The education service is also required to have individuals designated to take on child protection responsibility, and the role of those individuals within schools and within the LEAs are described. Education representatives tend to rely on written material and training to disseminate information generally, although child protection training for education staff is problematic.

4 Being a member of an Area Child Protection Committee

An Area Child Protection Committee is no more or less than its members. This does not simply mean that without its members there can be no committee; or even the more substantive point that this particular committee, unlike some, does not have an established apparatus which would continue to function even if the committee itself were inactive. Rather, the essence of an Area Child Protection Committee is that it is constituted of people who are representatives of particular kinds of organisations, holding particular kinds of positions within those organisations, and with particular knowledge, skills and experience. Many committees could function, even if not very effectively, if they were composed of a random group of people (some even appear to be just that). However, if the Area Child Protection Committee did not consist of the right people it would not fulfil its purpose at all.

The knowledge and experience, the understanding and commitment, the individual strengths and weaknesses that members bring to the committee, are likely to play a large part in determining how the committee defines and approaches its tasks and how effectively it carries them out. Members are typically middle managers or senior practitioners from the agencies represented on the committee. They will usually have had substantial experience of practice themselves before taking on responsibility for the practice of others. How far does this experience prepare them for their role in representing their agency on the Area Child Protection Committee?

This chapter considers the membership of Area Child Protection Committees. We will look at what agencies the members represent, how regularly they attend, and how this affects the balance of the committees. We will consider who chairs and convenes the committees and the implications of this for the activity of the committees. We will look at the subjects discussed in committee meetings and how this reflects the priorities of the committees. We will look at how members go about representing their agencies on the committees. We begin, however, by looking at the simple question of the size of committees. How many members are there and what effect does size have on the functioning of the committees?

How many members are there?

Table 4.1 shows the total membership of each of the eight Area Child Protection Committees in Wales at the time we conducted our research. It shows a membership varying between 18 and 31 members, apart from one committee with an atypically small membership of 10. Apart from this exception, the committees seemed to divide into two groups: a group of four with between 18 and 20 members, and a group of three with between 26 and 31 members. The average size of membership was between 21 and 22 (whether or not we exclude the lowest and highest). It seems probable that this pattern of size of membership is fairly typical of England and Wales generally.

Table 4.1
Size of Area Child Protection Committees in Wales

ACPC	Size
A	28
B	10
C	19
D	19
E	18
F	31
G	26
H	20

The variation is related to the number of agencies represented on each committee. The larger committees tended to include agencies in addition to those recommended in *Working Together*. Examples of these are voluntary organisations (both local and national), groups representing cultural or religious interests, and professionals not normally included in child protection arrangements such as school dentists. On the other hand, the smaller committees often left out one or more of the recommended representatives, for example teachers and general practitioners, or those not recommended in guidance but included in many committees such as the local authority solicitor. In the case of the exceptionally small committee there had been a deliberate decision taken to keep the numbers low as it was believed that a smaller committee would be more effective.

What sort of people are they?

For the most part the committee members are relatively senior professionals. Many of them occupy middle management roles in their agencies although some are better described as senior managers. In both cases, however, they usually have a clear *professional* identity as nurses, social workers, police officers, teachers, and so on. Some members are primarily practitioners although their status may still be relatively senior. Doctors often fall into this category, as sometimes do psychologists and lawyers. A number of those we interviewed indicated that their direct experience of work with children and families, and that of their colleagues from other agencies on the committee, often constituted their best qualification for being a member and the best assurance that they would do the job well.

If our sample is representative, and it probably is reasonably so at least in Wales and at least as far as the main agencies are concerned, the members are for the most part men, as shown in Table 4.2.

Table 4.2
Area Child Protection Committee representatives interviewed: agency and sex

Agency	Male	Female
Social Services	5	3
Health - Nursing	-	2
Health - Medical	7	1
Education - LEA	3	2
Education - Headteacher	4	-
Police	7	1
Probation	1	-
Others	-	2
Total	27	11

Our sample also indicates wide variations between agencies in the length of service of committee members. On average, health service representatives had been on the committee longest, with an average of 7.8 years. Representatives from the education service were next, with 4.6 years. Social services followed with 3.7 years, and finally the police with only 2.3 years on average. In view of our findings concerning the relative domination of committee business by social services and the police, (see 'ACPC agendas' below and 'Levels of involvement' in chapter 5), it is interesting that in general the representatives of those agencies appear to be relative newcomers in comparison with their numerous colleagues from the health and education services who may have been attending the committee for twice as long.

Which agencies do members represent?

Table 4.3 shows which agencies the 171 members of the eight committees represented. The majority came from the health service (35 per cent) or the social services department (24 per cent). In the case of social services, this reflects the lead responsibility that social services departments carry (and the fact that the chair and convenor are usually social services personnel - see below). In the case of health, it reflects the diverse structure of the health service, with its multiple lines of accountability which mean that one or two people cannot effectively represent all relevant interests as can be done, for example, by the police. This has always been the case in the health service because of the way in which medical and nursing services are divided between specialisms and between hospital and community services, but it has now been greatly accentuated by the purchaser-provider split and the proliferation of trusts (see chapter 7).

Table 4.3
ACPC membership by agency

Agency	Total membership
Health	60
Social Services	41
Education	21
Police	14
Probation	11
Others	24
Total	**171**

Education representatives accounted for 24 per cent of total membership, and the police for only 8 per cent, although this is unlikely to be a true reflection of their importance in the committees. Probation had 6 per cent of total membership (which still represents on average more than one probation representative per committee) and the remaining 14 per cent came from a variety of other agencies including the voluntary sector.

Although the health service was heavily represented, there were still difficulties in ensuring that certain services had a member speaking for them on the committee. This applied particularly to general practitioners. We were offered a number of explanations for this absence: a lack of commitment to child protection or to interagency work on the part of GPs, a lack of funding for attendance at meetings when GPs tend to expect payment for such activities, or a feeling that because GPs are independent contractors one GP cannot represent the views or interests of others (apart from his or her own immediate colleagues and partners). This seems to us an important point. The Area Child Protection Committee is dominated by people working in more or less hierarchical management structures, and very often occupying management positions within those structures. They tend to be confident, within limits, in their ability to speak for an organisation and those working within it, and to make or refuse commitments on behalf of others. None of these characteristics apply to GPs who stand in a very different relationship to their colleagues and to the organisation which engages their services; and it would be surprising if this did not create both practical difficulties and misunderstandings. The same applies to some extent to school teachers. Head teacher representatives often said to us that they felt unable to represent colleagues other than staff of their own school. At the same time representatives from education authorities referred to their inability to direct what happened in schools.

There were some categories of membership which were common to all eight committees. Every committee included a paediatrician, a child psychiatrist and a nursing manager. Every committee included a senior social services manager as well as the child protection coordinator. Every committee included a representative of the local education authority. Every committee included a senior police officer and representatives of the probation service and the NSPCC. These points of consistency closely reflect the government's recommendations in *Working Together* regarding composition of Area Child Protection Committees. Beyond this, however, there was a great deal of variation in membership, only some of which appeared to us to reflect real local differences in circumstances.

On the other hand, there were a number of roles which occurred only once among the 171 committee members. There was one clinical psychologist, one police surgeon, one magistrates' clerk, one crown prosecutor, one member of a race equality council and one representative of a school medical service. In some cases these people had been taken on in order to perform a particular task. The psychologist for example was leading a sub-group to look at treatment for victims of child abuse. In other cases the lone member seemed to represent an emergent trend; for instance, a number of committees were considering inviting a representative of the Crown Prosecution Service, although only one had actually done so at the time of our research.

Working Together recommends that committees should 'establish links' with organisations who may have a contribution to make to improving child protection services. There is room for debate about whether that implies including representatives on the main committee or making links through some other mechanism - whether that be informal, through personal contacts or occasional meetings, or formal, through subcommittees. It is worth noting that the largest committee in our study was the one which had no district committee structure. The implication of this is that perhaps more of the work that would be covered in district committees in other ACPCs is being covered in the main committee necessitating a larger attendance to ensure local input and feedback. To keep the main ACPC more streamlined, it could be argued that a more effective structure would be to have links with other organisations at local level, and those interests could then be represented at ACPC via the District Child Protection Committees. The work of subcommittees is discussed more fully in Chapter 5.

Who attends the committee meetings?

Table 4.4 shows the actual attendance (as a percentage of possible attendance) over six consecutive meetings, compared to the membership of each committee.

Table 4.4
ACPC Attendance

Area	A	B	C	D	E	F	G	H
Number of members	28	10	19	19	21	31	26	21
Percentage attendance	45%	93%	59%	65%	55%	46%	57%	58%

The proportion of members attending meetings has a very strong negative correlation with the number of members ($r = -0.9$). The smaller committees achieve a higher percentage attendance whilst the larger committees have considerably lower percentage attendance. This lends some support to the argument made during interview with the chair of the smallest committee (Area B), that greater effectiveness would result from keeping the numbers low. This committee in fact achieved the highest level of attendance. One may conjecture that this is partly because of the greater extent of involvement members have in the proceedings when committees are smaller. Certainly the lowest percentage attendances recorded were for the two largest committees, which suggests either that attendance was not very stable or consistent, or that some people who were nominally members very seldom attended.

In fact our discussions with members suggested that the answer was perhaps a bit of both, in that there was a 'hard core' of members who nearly always attended, a larger number who attended perhaps one in two or two in three meetings, and finally a small minority who hardly ever attended. The 'hard core' naturally included the chair and the child protection coordinator. In addition, senior police representatives attended on 86 per cent of possible occasions, and nursing managers on 70 per cent. On the other hands some representatives clearly fell into the 'less frequent attender' category, including head teachers and child psychiatrists (both 47 per cent overall) and general practitioners (38 per cent overall). It appeared that professionals who were most closely involved with prevention or treatment of abuse, as opposed to investigation of alleged abuse, were the least likely to attend meetings.

Who chairs the committee meetings?

The normal practice in England and Wales is for the Area Child Protection Committee to be chaired by a senior manager of the social services department. This is not required in *Working Together*, although the guidance does imply that it will be the norm. However, it expressly provides that the committee may be chaired by someone else if the agencies agree, although it recommends that in this case the vice-chair should be a senior officer of the social services department. In only one of the areas we studied had this happened. In this case it had been agreed that a senior representative of the health service should chair the committee. This had been done on the suggestion of the director of social services, because the committee was engaged in enquiring into serious matters for which that officer had managerial responsibility. It was expected that, after those enquiries had been completed, the chair of the committee would in due course revert to the social services department.

In the other seven areas the committee was chaired by a senior manager of the social services department; either the director of social services or the deputy director, or an assistant director with responsibility for services to children. This was generally regarded as being the expected arrangement, and remarkably little attention had been paid to the recommendation in the Cleveland Inquiry (Butler-Sloss, 1988) that the responsibility for chairing the committee should rotate between agencies from time to time.

'Fitting in' to the committee

The picture we have, then, is of committees which are dominated numerically, at least on paper, by representatives of the health service and of the social services department, but where in practice it is rare for more than half the membership to attend any meeting. On the other hand a few key personnel attend virtually every meeting. What is the effect of this on the balance and flavour of discussion, and the decisions taken, at what is meant to be the principal coordinating body for all the agencies involved in child protection services?

Comments by a number of those we interviewed suggested that the discussion at the meetings tended to reflect the concerns of those seen as the principal attenders ('key players' as one of them put it). This referred to the social services representatives, who also drew up the agenda, and the agencies such as police, nursing and paediatric services who were frequently involved in the investigation of alleged abuse. Later on we suggest that there may be an element of circularity in that subjects discussed at the meeting come to reflect the concerns of the principal attenders. Other members told us how hard it could be for a new or infrequent attender to make their views known, or even to understand what was going on, at meetings dominated by a relatively small number of people who knew each other and where discussion often returned to the same issues at one meeting after another. We consider below the ways in which new members are briefed as to their roles and responsibilities, and it may be that inadequacies in this process contribute to such feelings of alienation. However, some responsibility must rest with those at the meeting, particularly those who attend regularly, to ensure that incomers are aware of what is going on and how they may intervene. Members told us of the friendliness of some meetings and of the warm welcome they received. Others, however, spoke of feeling excluded by the atmosphere of the meeting in different ways. One woman on a mainly-male committee described it as 'rather like the rugby club'!

Becoming a member

Membership of an Area Child Protection Committee is a responsible position. Area Child Protection Committees are accountable for the procedures followed in responding to child abuse and neglect and have specific obligations to review the most serious cases (described in chapter 8). Membership normally entails being a representative of an agency, and therefore members have to combine their duties as a member of the area committee with their responsibilities to and on behalf of their own agencies. In undertaking our research we considered how committee members understood their task, and how they prepared themselves for it.

Those interviewed were asked how they were introduced to their role as ACPC representatives. We were searching for some type of formal briefing from within the agency to ensure that representatives understood their responsibilities, what was expected of them, and the level of their authority as representatives. In fact we found an almost universal absence of any formal briefing. Some members had been informally briefed by their predecessors, and some recalled an initial discussion with the Chair of the committee. Others on the other hand, said that they wished that they had been offered a discussion with the Chair on commencing their duties. Most significantly however, almost no one recalled being informed by a senior manager in their own agency as to their responsibilities or their delegated authority as a representative on the ACPC.

One or two representatives, notably from social services, said that they had felt quite well briefed at their first meeting of the ACPC; and more recently appointed members tended to recall being better briefed than others who were appointed some years ago. This may be an indication that practice is improving in this respect, and at least one member told us that they themselves had been inadequately briefed but that practice had now improved. However, it may also be that in some cases more recent events are more clearly remembered. The general picture is of briefings which, to the extent that they take place at all, appear to be inadequate or perfunctory. This may explain why some respondents were hazy as to whether they had been through a process of introduction or not. For instance one member said to us: 'I don't think I've been

47

briefed, actually.' It was clear that this respondent had had to form his own understanding of what his responsibilities were, and that this had taken some time. Another respondent confessed to finding the experience quite 'daunting' at first; there was no induction and it had taken time to feel comfortable. However, this member also indicated that he had learned quickly that the committee was not very active, and that a few people did most of the work in sub-groups. Many committee members, even those who had been in office for some time, confessed that they remained uncertain about aspects of their role. In part this may be attributed to the absence of clear expectations from their management. In no case did we find a written description of the responsibilities of an ACPC representative.

This lack of briefing means that members usually have to work out for themselves what their role is, and to some extent what the functions of the committee are (although this is at least written down in *Working Together*). As meetings usually only take place between four to six times per year, representatives often describe a period of about twelve to eighteen months before they begin to feel comfortable as a member of the ACPC, and able to contribute effectively. Given the turnover in membership this probably means that at any one time up to a quarter of the members of the committee are, at least in their own view, operating in a very limited way. It also suggests that there is considerable potential for misunderstandings both within and between agencies about the extent of the authority which representatives may have to enter into agreements on behalf of their agencies and to commit their agencies to particular courses of action. In addition, there may be a frequent need for agreements reached at the Area Child Protection Committee to be ratified by senior managers or other decision-making systems within agencies. This indeed we found to be the case.

The process of representation

For most committee members representation is a two-way process. On the one hand they are expected to contribute to the development of policy, speaking on behalf of their agencies. This means that they are not simply expressing a personal view. They will need to be familiar with the position their agency wishes to take on a variety of issues, not merely those which are already on the agenda but, to be fully effective, a whole range of issues which may come up unexpectedly from time to time. On the other hand, they are also expected to take policy back to their agencies and to ensure that it is implemented. They represent the Committee to their agencies as well as representing their agencies' view to the Committee. The effectiveness with which they are able to do this depends in part on how closely they are in touch with colleagues with whom they can discuss child protection matters.

We asked our respondents how they found out what colleagues in their own agencies thought about issues which came before the committee. It was clear that many Committee members take considerable steps to ensure that they are in touch with colleagues' views on subjects which are likely to need discussion or decision. How did representatives from the different agencies strive to achieve this? *Social services* members, who were usually employed as child protection coordinators and therefore unlike most members of Committees spent most of their time working on child protection matters, used a number of different methods for keeping in touch. These included regular discussion with the Committee Chair, (who was normally a senior manager in social services), making themselves available to social work staff who needed to consult them on issues of policy or practice, participation in a range of child protection meetings involving junior managers and practitioners, such as district committees or meetings with independent conference chairs, participation in social services management forums (for example, children and family management team meetings), involvement in training programmes and in exceptional cases managing child protection workers. Only one of the coordinators we interviewed did not feel they had reliable contact with current views in their Department.

In contrast, *education* representatives often felt that they were not in close touch with the group they represented, and did not have a clear mandate. This was true not only for headteachers, but also for representatives of the education authority. In both groups individuals referred to informal telephone contact with colleagues, but there was little sign of more formal mechanisms, although there were exceptions. One head teacher commented, 'I'm not satisfied that I do represent my colleagues effectively. I'd like a mechanism that allows me to do it in a more structured way'. Education representatives tended to feel isolated from each other as well as from other colleagues in their offices or schools.

Health service representatives seemed to be generally satisfied with their ability to represent the views of colleagues. Whilst this may not necessarily apply on every single issue as it arises, they generally felt in touch with the general views of colleagues through meetings and training. They considered it important that colleagues felt able to contact them freely if there were issues which concerned them. Some health representatives clearly saw themselves as representing more than one interest. For example,

> I am not expected, as a specialist, simply to be a mouthpiece; I am expected to express some personal views. I keep in mind what the health authority's responsibility might be, in terms of the mental health element of child protection, and also the view of colleagues here, and also what the body of child psychiatrists in the country might be saying.

For general practitioners, the process of representation is similar. They do not necessarily know the views of other GPs on every issue that comes up, but rather try to ensure that local GPs know who to contact if they have anxieties about a child protection issue. There is concern to get it right, so that representatives do not find themselves agreeing to something that colleagues would find untenable. In some cases a representative might take an issue to the Local Medical Committee (LMC) to seek a representative view (bearing in mind that the LMC may be a committee of 40 representing a community of 200-300 general practitioners). The general practitioner representative to the ACPC should, in accordance with *Working Together*, be a member of the LMC.

Police representatives pay considerable attention to consistency of representation, and to questions of authority. Police representatives appeared to have exceptionally clear perceptions of these issues, and the clearest structures guiding representation on the Area Child Protection Committees. Some respondents were from senior police management, and others from Family Support Units. Senior officers tended to have close contact with an Assistant Chief Constable and with other branches of the Force. Family Support Units are small enough for staff to be in regular contact with each other and be aware of others views.

The authority of representatives

Working Together advises that ACPC appointees 'should have sufficient authority to allow them to speak on their agencies' behalf and to make decisions to an agreed level without referral to the appointees' agencies. The level of decision making delegated to appointees needs to be considerable to enable ACPCs to operate effectively' (paragraph 2.8). In practice this may depend on whether the committee is seen as an advisory or as an executive body, an issue identified by some of those interviewed.

We asked respondents to give an example of an issue on which they would be able to agree or to act as an ACPC representative on their own authority, and an example of an issue on which they would need to refer back to their agency. In general, respondents thought they could agree or act upon decisions about matters of practice, training, and production of guidance or information leaflets. They could not commit their agencies to policy changes or financial decisions. This may be associated with the difficulties that ACPCs have in securing budgets or to the more general increasingly tighter constraints over expenditure in recent years. Although there were differences between agencies, this was a very consistent pattern of response.

Representatives may be able to consult with more senior colleagues on matters coming up in the ACPC. Often, however, there will be insufficient time after the agenda appears for such consultations to take place in time for the meeting. This means that one effect of lack of authority may be to delay the process of decision making, with the risk that important issues will get lost. It appears that changes within agencies may have made it more difficult to get decisions on some issues, as we note in chapter 7.

Some representatives, for instance, general practitioners and headteachers, do not represent 'agencies' as such. In these cases the nature of authority is very different. Several respondents suggested that formal position was not in any case the best or only measure of a member's level of authority: 'What we're looking for is people who have the respect within their agency to ensure that what they agree will be accepted'.

The ACPC agenda

All respondents were asked if they had put an item on the ACPC agenda over the preceding twelve months. The objective of this question was to assess the extent to which members saw their role on the ACPC as proactive or whether, for whatever reasons, they were content to let others set the agenda and simply contribute to the discussion of issues as they arose. The results indicated that the most active contributors to the ACPC agendas are social services and the police. All but one of the social services representatives had put an item on the agenda during the preceding twelve months, and for the police, five of the eight had. By contrast, the two least active contributors are headteachers and general practitioners. Of three general practitioners interviewed, none had put an item on the agenda. Of four headteachers, only one had.

Respondents were also asked if they would discuss items on the ACPC agenda before the meeting, either within their agency, or with colleagues in other agencies. For example, headteachers were asked to consider if they would discuss the ACPC agenda with other teachers in their school, or with headteachers in other schools. In general, apart from Child Protection Coordinators (who compile the agenda), most representatives indicated that they did not formally or informally discuss ACPC agendas before the meetings. This may be a reflection that for the other ACPC members child protection is not likely to take up a large proportion of their work, and therefore does not receive a great deal of emphasis in the workplace. The fact that most do not discuss agenda issues however, in conjunction with our earlier consideration of the lack of briefing of representatives conveys an impression of ACPC members being relatively isolated in their role.

Personal views on effectiveness of representation

We asked each respondent if they felt they were the right person to represent their agency on the Area Child Protection Committee. We made it clear to each respondent that we were asking them about their position within the organisation and not about their personal qualities. However, some respondents did choose to refer to personal skills, knowledge and background, or to how they were perceived by colleagues. Some members of an ACPC are there *ex officio*, such as child protection coordinators from social services, and for them the question of whether they were the most appropriate person seemed redundant. On the other hand, even for some child protection coordinators the question served to highlight an element of uncertainty about how they were perceived within their own agency. The majority of police representatives considered that they were the right people to be representing the Force on the committee. We also found that health service representatives were all satisfied that they were the right people to be representatives.

In education, on the other hand, there was a difference between local education authority representatives and headteachers. Most LEA representatives felt that they were not in the right position to represent the agency, and for some this was a strongly held view. Headteacher respondents all felt that there should be a headteacher representative, although some individuals expressed misgivings about whether they were any more qualified than any other headteacher to be that representative.

We also asked members if they considered that the representatives from other agencies on their committee were the right people to be doing that job. The patterns of response to this question were rather different. The police and social services representatives were in general quite dissatisfied with the representation from other agencies, while health and education representatives were relatively satisfied. This pattern may be related to the different levels of involvement in the process of managing child protection. It may not be coincidental that the highest levels of dissatisfaction were being expressed by representatives of the two agencies that (a) appear to have very close working relationships with each other and (b) are most closely involved in the investigative work which lies at the heart of present ACPC concerns.

In addition, a number of representatives also referred positively to the representation from the National Society for the Prevention of Cruelty to Children (NSPCC) as well as voluntary agencies such as Barnardos and National Children's Home (NCH Action for Children).

Interagency relationships

The discussion of ACPC representatives' estimation of effectiveness of other agencies' representation leads to the issue of interagency relationships more generally. Nearly every inquiry since that into the death of Maria Colwell (Department of Health and Social Security, 1974a) has highlighted poor communications or interagency difficulties as a contributing factor to the breakdowns resulting in the death of children. At times relationships between the different professions with responsibilities for child protection can be very strained indeed. For example, Weightman (1988) reports a general practitioner as saying 'social workers are worse than useless, they are positively dangerous', and a headteacher's comment that 'in five minutes a social worker can undo five years work in winning parental support'. Although the quality of interagency relationships in Wales varies, we can report that nowhere did we find anything approaching that kind of contempt or distrust. In fact overall, we found that interagency working relationships appeared to be rather more positive than had been expected.

It is widely accepted today that agencies must work together, and that open communication and sharing of information will most effectively protect children. It is often assumed that close working relationships between senior managers of different agencies will foster the development of good, open working practices at field level. However, this may not always follow. The report of the Liam Johnson inquiry (London Borough of Islington, 1989) commented: 'We are left with an overwhelming impression of a talking shop in which there is a good level of rapport and co-operation between the individuals who comprise the ACPC and its subcommittees, but the agencies whom they represent continue largely to perform their task in ignorance of these deliberations and achievements' (para 9.4). We do not know of any attempt to test empirically the degree of correspondence between interagency relationships at management and at field level.

We wondered whether good relationships on the ACPC might coexist with poor relationships in the field, and vice versa. Clearly interviews with practitioners would be necessary to test these propositions with any degree of thoroughness. However we thought it worthwhile to explore the perceptions our respondents held, not only of the relationships between colleagues from different agencies on the ACPC, who are mostly managers, but also of the working relationships which they believed existed between practitioners from the several agencies. This of course often included the practitioners whom they managed or who would consult them about difficult cases; so it is arguable that they would be likely to see poor instances of collaboration disproportionately often, and this should be borne in mind when interpreting what we found.

In fact we found a very high positive correlation between the *perceived* strength of relationships between particular agencies in the ACPC and in the field. In most cases the ACPC relationship between agencies was seen as stronger than the field relationships. A number of factors may account for this. First, some ACPC members are in very frequent contact, with informal contact between meetings and contact through district committees and subcommittees. Second, working together on common objectives, such as the development of local procedures manuals, may bring members closer together. Reder, Duncan and Gray (1993, p.129) observe that this task 'involves more than the act of writing by each committee representative. One agency's guidelines have to be compatible with those of all other agencies and, therefore, the ability of professionals to work together and implement the procedures depends on resolution of any differences between agencies'. Third, as we suggested above, it is possible that the impression of working relationships at practice level which ACPC members form is distorted by their role as managers in resolving conflicts and disagreements, while they see less of the situations where field relationships are working well.

Surprisingly, the relationship between the police and social services did not turn out to be the strongest one at ACPC level, although it was at field level. This was a surprise because of impression gained during the interview stage of very strong alliances between the police and social services within the ACPC, as described both by themselves and by other agencies. Although the police tend to see their relationship with social services as the strongest one, social services representatives seem to see the relationship with the police as less strong than their relationship with colleagues in the health service. Sanders et al (1996b) have described more fully the relationships between the police and other agencies in the context of managing child protection services.

The relationship between education and the other agencies, at both field and ACPC level, was perceived to be the weakest. A number of factors may account for these views. They may be related to the changes in education, described in chapter 7. They may be related to the interagency tensions produced when ACPCs attempt to address the difficult issue of professional abuse. For example, two of the twenty-one Part 8

Reviews in the study by Colton et al (1996) involved longstanding cases of sexual abuse of pupils by teachers, in two different Welsh ACPCs. Or they may be related to the emphasis in Area Child Protection Committees on investigative processes, in which the role of education agencies is much less compared with the police, social services, and health. This last point may also be one reason why the relationship between social services and the police is so strong.

In general, however, we established that, at least as seen from the top, good ACPC relationships are associated with good field relationships, and poor ACPC relationships are associated with poor field relationships. This should not, of course, be taken to imply any particular causal explanation.

The effect of organisational change

We found again and again that it was impossible to ignore the impact of organisational change within the agencies constituting the ACPCs. We learned early on, and were repeatedly reminded, that this was an issue high on the agenda for all our respondents. The health service had been through a series of fundamental restructuring processes which had left many professionals very confused about their responsibilities, and whose effects were continuing. The education service was in a similar position because of reforms to the management of schools, and education, like social services, was faced with the prospect of local government reorganisation.

At the time when we carried out our research all the Welsh counties were facing reorganisation into a smaller number of unitary authorities. A similar process was going on in both England and Scotland at the same time, but in a much more variable and even spasmodic way. Although the commissioning group did not want us to concentrate on issues to do with the coming restructuring, we frequently found ourselves stubbing our toe on them, if only because the nature of the coming reorganisation raised some fundamental questions about the constitution of ACPCs which neither we nor our respondents could ignore. These issues are discussed further in chapter 7.

Summary

Chapter 4 has looked at the membership of Area Child Protection Committees and at the process of representation. We found that there is considerable variation in size of the committees, with some committees being three times the size of others. Some members have a high level of managerial experience, while others are there because of considerable practice experience. Men outnumber women by morme than two to one. The largest number of representatives on committees are from the health service, followed by social services, education, police, and probation. Attendance at committees varies from 45 per cent to 93 per cent of possible attenders, and smaller committees were observed to have a higher percentage attendance. Attendance was also considered to be related to the nature of the member agencies and their roles. The committees are almost invariably chaired by social services representatives.

We found that members had very little briefing on their responsibilities, although practice may be improving. We explored how representatives from the different agencies find out what the views of their colleagues are, and how they transmit those views to the ACPC and pass information about ACPC decisions to their colleagues. We asked what types of decisions members could make without referring back to their agencies, and what types of decisions they felt would need a more explicit mandate from the agency. We then looked at the agendas of ACPC meetings, and found that police and social services are the main contributors. We also found that only social services representatives seemed to liaise with colleagues in order to discuss agenda items before ACPC meetings. We then looked at how effectively agencies perceive other agencies to be represented, and how strong they perceive the relationships between agencies to be. The chapter finishes with a brief consideration of members' anxiety about the impact of past and future organisational changes: a subject which will be dealt with more fully in chapter 7.

5 How Area Child Protection Committees work

One of the key indicators of the effectiveness of an Area Child Protection Committee is how effective its formal meetings are. What do committee members think of the conduct of the meetings they attend? In general the comments of those we spoke to were fairly positive. Many talked to us of how the discussions at ACPC meetings improved the levels of mutual understanding and cooperation between personnel from different agencies. Several times this was described to us in terms of a steady process of 'team-building'. Other members referred with approval to a network of colleagues in different agencies who worked together informally as a direct result of their joint membership of the Area Child Protection Committee.

One of our informants, after talking with feeling about inter-professional rivalry, commented that 'One of the joys of being on the ACPC is to see that suspicion visibly reducing.' Others spoke of their appreciation for the friendliness shown at most meetings, and even more for the commitment shown by members to attending those meetings and to tackling some very difficult issues. This was not universal however. At least one respondent thought that the discussion tended to avoid sensitive issues, and that amicable relationships between members were preserved at the expense of tackling aspects of practice which really needed to be confronted. In general, however, the prevailing view is summed up by the comment 'We're all there for one reason, for the aim of better protecting children.'

Many members spoke very positively about how efficiently committee meetings were conducted, and in particular to how well they were chaired. It was clear that the chairpersons of Area Child Protection Committees enjoyed a great deal of personal respect; members referred to the open, honest and straightforward way in which discussions were led and business moved forward. Members also spoke approvingly of the agenda papers as being clear and comprehensible and circulated sufficiently in advance to allow at least some preparation to take place. There were a number of positive comments on the quality of discussion at the meetings (although there was also one very negative comment).

However, several of those we spoke to thought that the meetings were slow and even tedious. Others commented on how meetings were dominated by a few members and that some others had very little to say or otherwise contribute. The balance of criticism however was more of those who did not contribute, rather than of those who dominated the proceedings. The latter appeared to be seen as needing to say as much as they did to ensure that essential business was dealt with.

Opinions varied on the quality of decision-making at the meetings. Some members thought that decisions were reached whenever necessary, while others thought that decisions were often avoided. We were informed that on occasions decisions were delayed because of a need to refer back to agencies. In the previous chapter we considered the question of mandates for ACPC representatives, and how far they have the authority to commit their agencies to particular proposals. It is clear that this is a subject on which there are going to be differences. Child protection coordinators commented that decisions were sometimes made without much thought for implementation, or with an assumption that 'someone' (usually by default the coordinator) would sort out the details. One child protection coordinator showed us a line-per-item list more than a page long of things he needed to do as a result of decisions taken at the last meeting.

Most members felt that there was sufficient time to deal with issues properly, but there were two who dissented from this view. However, it did appear that there was considerable variation in the length of meetings. One of our respondents spoke of meetings in the past having been concluded in as little as fifteen minutes, while others told us of meetings lasting for several hours (in addition to whole-day sessions on topics of special interest). The frequency of meetings varied less, usually between four and six times per year.

The Chair's view

We talked to the committee chairs specifically about their view of how their committees worked. In general they too were pleased with the conduct of meetings and thought that business was effectively dealt with, although in most cases they considered that there was room for improvement. We asked them particularly about the committees' work in developing policy. We did this by asking each Chair three specific questions. First, we asked them to tell us, as an example, how the policy of parental participation in case conferences was developed in their area. Second, we asked whether there were other areas of policy which they had successfully developed, and what the difficulties had been. Third, we asked them for examples of areas of policy which they had wanted to develop but had not been able to do so.

In relation to parental participation in case conferences, the policy had usually been instituted several years prior to our research. In some cases this meant that the policy had already been in place when the Chair we spoke to had been appointed. Others suggested that since the guidance from government on parental participation was fairly prescriptive, there was little choice for committees in how to implement it. However, others told us that there had been considerable resistance to the policy which had needed to be overcome before it could be effectively implemented. Such resistance could be explicit at the level of policy formulation, or could take the form of de facto resistance to its implementation. For instance, in one area there had been a formal policy to allow parental participation for a number of years, but very few parents actually attended conferences. As one respondent put it, 'there are ways to avoid the imperative to involve parents'. This seems to be an example of how a gap can emerge between policy and practice. People who in organisational terms are fairly close to practice can agree a policy which then appears to have very little impact on what actually happens.

Some Chairs thought that monitoring needed to be introduced in order to prevent such a gap emerging. Others spoke of the importance of including an element of research in the development of a policy such as that on parental participation, and of their frustration when this was not possible. On the other hand, in one case the progress of the policy on parental participation in conferences was considered to have been held back by the need to await the results of initial research. Other Chairs talked to us of the importance of introducing training into the development of the policy, in order to ensure that misgivings were properly aired and that all agencies and professions had the chance to move forward together.

There were a host of other areas in which committee chairs told us they had successfully developed policy. These included:

- Local child protection procedures
- Joint work between the police and social services
- Policies on invitations to case conferences
- Information for attenders at case conferences
- Parental suicide attempts involving children
- Information monitoring
- Commissioning of video interview suites
- Issues involving minority communities
- Genital mutilation
- Organised abuse
- Abuse by professionals
- Use of family group conferences
- Disseminating information about child protection in schools, and
- Services to children in need

What many of the above items have in common is an emphasis on issues around investigation and case conferences. Only two appear to address issues specifically related to prevention - children in need, and work in schools (the latter concerned sponsorship of a theatre production aimed at teenagers about the issue of sexual abuse, which was considered a success). Significantly, none of the items mentioned appears to be concerned with treatment or after-care for abused children and their families. The important issue of the balance between prevention, investigation and treatment in the management of child protection services is one to which we will return.

The areas of policy where committee chairs felt that they had not made as much progress as they would have liked included a wider range of matters. We had thought that chairs might indicate areas where disagreement had prevented progress. In fact they tended to tell us about work which they would have liked to have done if their committee had had sufficient time, which may mean that this list says something about what the committees would be doing in an ideal world. For instance prevention was identified as needing much more attention - and not just prevention targeted at high-risk groups. One example given was the creative use of the media as part of a child abuse prevention strategy. Likewise, treatment services were clearly regarded as being in need of development, and two committee chairs talked specifically of their difficulties in developing policies for the treatment of abusers. It appeared that some agency representatives regard this as a diversion from the main task of preventing children being abused.

The narrow view taken of committees' responsibility for developing treatment and aftercare services is a recurring theme in our research (see for example Sanders et al, 1996a), and members' views of this are discussed later in this chapter. In one committee treatment for child victims was only considered insofar as it related to children who abuse other children. Neither follow-up and harm reduction for children who have been abused, nor counselling for partners of abusers were mentioned to us as policy areas which might be developed in the future. While preventative services are neglected in practice but at least appear on the 'wish lists' of child protection committees, it appears that treatment services are absent even from their dreams. When we asked about the reasons why treatment policies might be underdeveloped, we were referred both to the lack of resources and to the attitudes of committee representatives.

Other aspects of policy which chairs would have liked to develop included:

- Training (where there appeared to be an expectation from other agencies that social services would provide all the training needed)
- Abuse by people outside the family (in two areas the committee chair indicated that the committee had not developed a policy or procedures on how to deal with extra-familial abuse), and
- Establishing of complaint and case review procedures.

Chairs made some interesting comments on the nature of some of the obstacles to desired policy development. In some instances this had to do with difficulties in getting agencies and professionals to agree on what the policy should be. In others, however, the difficulties were more to do with the process of policy formation. Chairs expressed the view that policies took too long to draft because of excessive 'perfectionism' on the part of subcommittees charged with the task. This may of course reflect a difference between two approaches to the management task, one being an 'executive' approach concerned with getting things done without delay, the other a more 'consensual' approach which is concerned with establishing the best possible basis for progress, particularly in interagency work.

Where is the main emphasis of the committees' work?

We were concerned that there appeared to be a considerable imbalance in the committees' activity between the areas of child protection policy identified in *Working Together* (paragraph 2.12) as their responsibility. These we have described as: (a) the investigation of alleged or suspected abuse, including the processes of case conference and registration/deregistration; (b) the prevention of abuse to children both within the family and from outside, including both prevention aimed at 'high-risk' groups and broader preventative efforts; and (c) treatment services, including specific therapy and more general after care for children who have suffered abuse and their families. Treatment services for abusers may be classified either as treatment, because practically that is what they are, or as prevention, because functionally that is how they operate in relation to future abuse.

In order to see whether our concern was reflected in child protection committee members' understanding of their work, we asked our respondents about their view of where their committees' concerns fell in relation to these areas of policy. Most of our respondents thought that their committees' emphasis was overwhelmingly on investigation. 'Investigation' was the word most commonly mentioned, along with 'procedures', 'identification', 'referral' and 'registration'. Indeed, several respondents appeared to equate child protection with these processes to the exclusion of anything else. Others took a wider view of child protection, and wanted to see the work of the committees reflect these wider concerns. One respondent suggested that in fact all child protection work should be seen in terms of prevention. This respondent used Hardiker's threefold classification of prevention, defining investigation and the use of the child protection register as secondary prevention, and treatment services as tertiary prevention.

Some members thought that their committees did devote some attention to prevention, or at least were beginning to do so. However, this was often seen largely in terms of educational projects encouraging earlier identification or referral, rather than in terms of services designed to reduce the incidence of abuse in the first place. Others thought that prevention was largely neglected because of the overriding emphasis on reacting to cases of identified abuse. In relation to treatment there was more general agreement that this was a neglected area of policy and of practice. An often-repeated comment was to the effect that 'nothing like enough attention' was given to treatment matters. A small number of respondents thought that this might be beginning to change.

We conducted a detailed analysis of the first 27 interviews in order to establish respondents' views as to the balance of emphasis between investigation, treatment and prevention. The transcripts were searched for statements in relation to four or five specific questions. In relation to the identified policy areas of (1) prevention, (2) investigation and registration, (3) treatment, we looked at whether the respondent considered that each area was dealt with satisfactorily by the committee. We then looked to see (4) whether the respondent seemed to be saying that there was an overwhelming emphasis on one area of policy. Where this was the expressed opinion, we also looked for statements which indicated (5) whether the respondent was happy with this situation. Using this method we were able to elicit answers to the first four questions in between 22 and 25 cases.

We found that 9 respondents thought that prevention was dealt with adequately, and 13 that it was not. By contrast, 25 clearly considered that investigation and registration were dealt with satisfactorily. On the other hand, 24 thought that treatment was not dealt with adequately, and only 1 took the view that it was. Overall, 19 respondents thought the overwhelming emphasis was on the policy for investigation and registration, and only 4 seemed to think that it was not.

Of the 19, 10 gave clear expressions of dissatisfaction with this situation. It was apparent that a number of our respondents wanted to see the committee take a broader approach to child protection policy and service strategy. Typical comments included:

> Until now on the investigation, rather than treatment. And that's been a gap. Our thinking is changing. We're saying we need to change the emphasis, but how we're going to move from here to there is another matter.

> Traditionally ACPCs... concentrated on registration and investigation; I don't think that sufficient consideration has been given either to the treatment or the prevention side... Because it is such an emotive issue. Society's first concern has been on the registration and investigation and on protecting.

> The child protection system in this country is very procedurally driven and led. The system looks at the sharp end, e.g. child protection, conferencing, etc. The work on prevention is often seen as the remit of health.

> The investigation - a lot of emphasis on that. I'd like to see more prevention, and I'd certainly like to see more help, treatment, therapy.

There were some interesting differences between agencies. The education and health representatives were most dissatisfied with the lack of attention given to prevention. However, all agencies were united in considering that investigation and registration were dealt with satisfactorily, and that treatment was not. When it came to the general view taken of the balance of policy, the sharpest difference was between the police and the other agencies. In general the police representatives did not express the view that there was an overwhelming emphasis on investigation and registration, and if they did they were not unhappy with it.

Many respondents, however, were frustrated at their inability to attend to primary prevention or treatment. In one area where this was particularly so, our respondents were asked to estimate what percentage of ACPC time was spent on each area of work, and all agreed that between 70 per cent and 90 per cent was devoted to procedures for investigation and registration. The view was expressed that whenever the committee tried to turn its attention to prevention or treatment, issues arose in relation to investigation which took priority. Often these were driven from outside, for instance with the publication of the Memorandum of Good Practice (Home Office/Department of Health, 1992).

Levels of involvement

It should be becoming clear by now that there may be very different levels of involvement in the management of the interagency protection of children, on the part of different agencies and their representatives. From our interviews with members of Area Child Protection Committees in Wales, it was clear that at least some representatives feel themselves and their agencies to be very much on the sidelines of the process. Conversely, some of the representatives we spoke to appeared to believe that some of their colleagues from other agencies were not as committed as they were. As one respondent put it, 'What we lack is an overall ownership of the process by agencies'.

Evans and Miller (1992) in their discussion of interagency collaboration suggested that a two tier system was beginning to emerge in ACPCs, with social services fieldwork staff and the police being in the first tier and the rest of the agencies in the second. While this analysis certainly has some relationship to what we found, it seems to us to oversimplify the situation in at least two ways. First, assigning agencies to one or other tier fails to take account of the extent to which levels of participation may vary according to local circumstances and to the attitudes of individuals. Second, a simple dichotomy does not seem to reflect fully the range of involvement which we observed.

We have discerned three different levels of 'ownership' of the process of managing the interagency protection of children. While there are clear patterns in the adoption by agencies of a greater or lesser level of participation, across the eight areas where we carried out our analysis there were some significant variations in these patterns. We describe the three levels below

Full 'Ownership'

Agencies at this level are involved in the whole range of subject matters considered by the committee, regardless of which agency may be most affected. Agencies taking full 'ownership' will assume responsibility for identifying issues which need to be considered by the committee and for planning and arranging for issues to be considered, as well as taking responsibility for the issues themselves. Such agencies also tend to assume leading roles in the main committee, in the district committees where they exist, and in the functional subcommittees - especially policy subcommittees and training subcommittees. This level of involvement is typically only fully demonstrated by social services departments.

Significant involvement

This is typical of agencies whose roles give them a high level of participation in the investigative process at an operational level. They therefore tend to play a significant role in the ACPCs, perhaps largely because the focus of ACPC considerations in recent years has been on the investigation and registration process. They are fully involved in issues around the procedures to be developed, and are likely to be strongly

62

represented in subgroups, such as policy and procedures subcommittees as well as on the main body of the ACPC. Agencies in this group are police, and some of the health agencies, for instance paediatricians.

Peripheral involvement

Representatives in this group consider issues under discussion largely from the perspective of whether or not they have specific relevance to their own agencies. We would not want to suggest that agencies or their representatives in this group do not take child protection seriously. It was clear from many comments made to us that they do. However, they do seem to regard their concerns as falling within this restricted range, and do not appear to have a sense of responsibility for the overall process. It is probably fair to say that the majority of members on a typical ACPC will fall into this category to a greater or lesser extent. However, within this group there is considerable variation in the actual degree of involvement. We would argue that this group frequently includes education (both LEA representatives and headteachers), probation, some health (for example general practitioners), as well as those other agencies who appear more or less often among the membership of ACPCs.

Variations in the level of involvement of different agencies or their representatives is often seen by colleagues in terms of different levels of commitment. Social services representatives to whom we spoke, and to a lesser extent police representatives, frequently expressed views about the relative lack of 'commitment' on the part of some agencies compared with others. It is certainly the case that agencies for whom child protection issues are not central to their work are likely to be less committed to the work of the ACPC than other agencies for whom these issues are more relevant. Similarly, professionals whose working role within their agency is so defined as to include a substantial concern with child protection are also likely to be more committed to the work of the committee than colleagues for whom child protection is not a major feature of their working day. However, it seemed to us that variations in the levels of involvement were also connected to the 'fragmentation' of some agencies, notably education and health who might have been expected to have a key role in child protection matters. In every ACPC we considered, the organisational changes within these agencies were identified as having had an impact on the nature of their participation in ACPCs.

When we interviewed the Chairs of the Welsh committees we sought to confirm our hypothetical model of three different levels of involvement in ACPC processes, which had emerged from our interviews with agency representatives. As Chairs have a coordinating role and operate at a strategic level within the ACPC, we anticipated that they might feel some resistance to the idea that there was differential involvement in, commitment to, or 'ownership' of the work of the committee. In fact, although there was some disagreement, most Chairs agreed that different degrees of commitment did exist. In every case the police and social services were seen as being at the heart of the process. Whilst there was some variation in how closely involved health representatives were seen to be (often depending upon which parts of the health service were being considered), education was frequently identified as being the agency least involved.

The perception of different levels of involvement is therefore shared both by members and by Chairs. This appears to result in frustration when individuals and agencies find themselves asking 'why is everyone else not as committed as we are?' It was frequently made clear to us that the variation is perceived as a reflection of agency role rather than a matter of personal commitment; and it rarely seemed to be associated with any personal animosity. At the same time it did not appear to us that anyone was addressing the root causes. On the one hand, we often saw people struggling to resolve or to manage the interagency problems that arise from different agencies having different levels of involvement, commitment and structures. On the other hand, we did not see people asking what could be done to share the 'ownership' of the work more evenly among participating agencies.

In addition to the specific organisational factors we have identified, it appears to us that the context in which there are such different levels of involvement is critically determined by two factors. The first is the identification of social services as 'lead' agency. The second is the overwhelming emphasis on investigation, case conferences and registration which we discuss elsewhere. Unless one is prepared to question these basic principles, it is unlikely that the less-involved agencies - which are often those in most direct contact with children - will become more central to the system.

Stevenson (1989) points out that the Department of Health failed to follow the suggestion in the Cleveland Inquiry that 'One way of ensuring a greater commitment would be for the chairmanship to rotate on a biennial basis between senior staff of the agencies involved reporting direct to each authority' (Butler-Sloss, 1988, p.54; cited in Stevenson, 1989, p. 180). As we noted earlier, only one of the eight ACPCs had a non-social services Chair at the time of our research, and the expectation was that this post too would eventually revert to a social services representative. For district committees, on the other hand, there seems to be a much greater willingness to allow other agencies to assume the role of Chair.

It is surely important to avoid child protection coming to be seen as an exclusively social services responsibility, or as a joint responsibility only between the police and social services. Even if one were to accept the present concentration on investigating and monitoring individual cases of abuse, it is clear that agencies such as health and education have critically important roles to play in that work. However, our argument is more fundamentally that the 'skewing' of interagency child protection work towards investigation and registration, and the frequent if not universal dominance of that work by certain agencies, are very closely connected.

The work of subcommittees

The efficiency of an Area Child Protection Committee depends in part on the systems and structures created to enable it to get through the large volume of work that needs to be dealt with. In most cases this involves the establishment of one or more subcommittees. If the main committee has too much business, the result can be long agendas, long meetings, more frequent meetings, and either a neglect of detail or a preoccupation with detail and a potential for failing to see the wood for the trees. On the other hand, if too much is delegated to subcommittees the result can be a loss of purpose for the main committee. The task, then, is to get the balance right.

We found that the ACPCs we studied used both functional subcommittees and geographically based district committees. Both have the purpose of enabling certain business to be dealt with in more detail than is possible for the ACPC. With functional committees this applies particularly to categories of work such as training, procedures or particular services or initiatives. In the ACPCs we studied, the number of such subcommittees ranged from two to seven. Some had clearly identified terms of reference. Others did not or else were not available when we did our research.

In total there were 26 functional subcommittees reporting to the eight ACPCs, an indication of their importance in getting the business done. Evidently a considerable amount of business is being done outside the ACPCs and being brought to ACPCs for consideration. But what business, exactly? For a start, all eight ACPCs had a training subcommittee, which planned or coordinated interagency child protection training. Four also had a policy and procedures subcommittee at the time of review, although it appeared that others had previously had such committees but had disbanded them once the local procedures handbook had been produced. Only two ACPCs had a media or publicity subcommittee.

Six of the eight had a case review or a review subcommittee; although this did not always mean the same thing in different ACPCs. In some cases this subcommittee was a vehicle for regularly reviewing the decisions of case conferences regarding registration of children. In other cases they were set up on an ad hoc basis, to coordinate the arrangements for a case review required under Part 8 of *Working Together* (see chapter 8). In at least one case, the review committee acted primarily as an appeal body for professionals, where there was disagreement about a decision. In other cases reviews were undertaken by district committees and there was no need for a specific case review subcommittee.

It is worth noting that in all eight areas there was only one prevention subcommittee and only one subcommittee addressing the treatment of children following abuse. This is consistent with the lack of attention paid to prevention and treatment which we found in other aspects of the committees' work.

District committees

District committees make it possible to give closer attention to local matters and to keep policy development informed by practice. Their membership often includes practitioners, or staff who are closer to practice than members of the main committee. The existence of district committees raised interesting issues about the functions of child protection committees and the relationship between policy, procedure and practice. They also pointed to some of the issues expected to emerge in the process of local government reorganisation. We therefore thought it worthwhile to look more closely at how the district committees were working and what they did.

Five of the ACPCs had functioning district committees at the time of the study. Two others had case review committees, which only looked at individual cases. The five discussed here also had wider responsibilities for policy or strategy. Broadly, committees were based on social services departments' geographical divisions, which in their turn were usually coterminous with district council boundaries. Each county therefore had three, four or five district committees, variously called 'district review committees' or 'district child protection committees'.

Some committees had very clear terms of reference which were set out in the procedures manual. In general these tended to concentrate on monitoring the quality of interagency work on referrals and identified cases, sorting out conflicts or misunderstandings between agency staff, and acting as a conduit for ACPC policy to permeate practice and for issues from practice to be brought to the attention of the main committee. Others were given more freedom to determine their own terms of reference. These sometimes paid more attention to service provision issues. Some committees were still adjusting to the transition from their previous role as local case committees. For instance, one still prefaced its minutes with a confidentiality statement, even though there was no discussion of cases recorded.

Membership of district subcommittees ranged from 14 to 27 members, usually first-line or middle managers from the constituent agencies. The relative distribution of agency representatives from the main agencies is consistent with that of the main committees, as shown by the average sizes given in table 5.1:

Table 5.1
Average District Child Protection Committee membership

Agency	Average Membership	Range
Health	6.5	3 - 11
Social Services	4.9	2 - 10
Education	2.5	1 - 5
Police	1.7	1 - 3
Probation	1.1	1 - 2
Others	2.9	-

All district committees had one, two or three additional members from 'other' agencies: the Crown Prosecution Service, the local housing authority, local defence establishments, and voluntary organisations (the NSPCC or Barnardos). Many individuals had dual, or even multiple, memberships. For example, one ACPC paediatrician also sat on all the district committees within the area. Most committees had some overlapping membership between district and main committee, and in one county the district chair was ex-officio a member of the main committee. Other members of district committees were also sent as delegates to the main committee, where they were expected to represent the district body rather than their own agency. There appeared to be only one ACPC which had a district committee structure without formal representation from DCPCs into the ACPC.

Overall, the attendance at DCPC meetings varies from 33 per cent to 78 per cent with an overall average attendance of 56 per cent; similar in fact to the level of attendance at the main committee. Committees were chaired for the most part by the social services manager for the area, although there were exceptions: paediatricians, a senior nurse, a senior probation officer, a head teacher. In one county all Chairs were from social services; in another none was. There is therefore more flexibility in choice of chairperson for these district committees than there is for a main Area Child Protection Committee.

We examined the most recent set of minutes for each district committee. Attendance varied from 7 members to 18, not always in proportion to the number on the membership list (see above). The subjects discussed were in some respects very consistent. All committees discussed the most recent minutes of the ACPC. This was often supported by additional feedback from a member who had been present. In most counties the district committee follows the same meeting cycle as the ACPC. The majority discussed the latest quarterly statistics, often in some detail.

About half the committees discussed cases, again in some detail. Some committees had a standing agenda item for case discussion, which was not always used. Others had a detailed report from the local social services manager, which might include a report on all new referrals, or even on a range of matters covering most of the business of the committee. Several committees discussed the ACPC annual report at the meeting whose minutes we saw. Fewer than half discussed training as a distinct subject, and in some districts this was under 'any other business' rather than as an agenda item. It may be, of course, that over a longer period more committees discuss training from time to time.

In general, district committees were regarded as working well, and as able to take on work that the main committee would not be able to do so effectively, if at all. The two way function was particularly valued. District committees feed into the ACPC from practice, and contribute to the development of policy. Although it is clear that they are not responsible for the creation of policy, at least two Chairs said that the ACPC would consult the district committees before introducing new policies or procedures. They are instrumental in coordinating operational child protection work, and in ensuring that ACPC policy is implemented at the local level. Their ability to support 'networking' at a local level was also seen as very useful.

District committees seem to function best in those counties where the main committee has a strong sense of corporate responsibility, where their tasks are clearly agreed and where their membership is defined in a way that gives them some authority. In one ACPC area where we were told of difficulties, these were attributed to the absence of clear terms of reference.

Financial arrangements

Clearly the activity of the Area Child Protection Committee will necessarily involve some financial costs. The extent of these costs are likely to vary according to the level and nature of that activity. Conversely, the ability of an ACPC to do what it wants to do may be enhanced or constrained by the financial resources available to it.

Working Together indicates that 'It will be the duty of the agencies represented on an ACPC to reach agreements on the budget the ACPC requires to accomplish the tasks which have been identified, and in order to support the work of the secretariat. Agencies should allocate funds to the ACPC in accordance with agreed arrangements at the beginning of each financial year so that the ACPC has an annual budget' (2.16) In other words, the responsibility lies with the constituent agencies to fund the work of the committee. However, the constituent agencies have very different levels of engagement with (and indeed legal responsibility for) child protection issues, and they also operate in very different financial circumstances although all have the task of setting priorities against restricted and often reduced budgets.

We were asked by the commissioning group at the Welsh Office to look at the question of budgets for the work of ACPCs. It was made clear to us that the information sought was in relation to the ACPC's own functions, and not to the resources devoted to child protection in general by agencies. In practice, however, the line between what is an agency's responsibility and what is an interagency responsibility may sometimes be a little difficult to draw, and it was apparent that this factor resulted in more than one instance in a divergence of opinion among the agencies represented on an Area Child Protection Committee.

We therefore looked at how ACPC budgets are created and how they are used. We found very large variations and considerable inconsistencies between different ACPCs, and even within the same ACPC on different occasions. In the first place, only three of eight ACPCs were able to supply us with written information about their budgets. From the three replies which we received, the total budget allocations for that year were apparently £62,000, £3,000, and nil. It is far from clear to us how to explain variations of this order of magnitude. In fact we understand that only two ACPCs in Wales have a specific budget of their own, although we have not been able to confirm this.

Further inconsistencies around budgeting issues emerged from our interviews. In the case of one ACPC, figures that were sent to us in advance did not match the figures which were supplied to us during the interview. In general there seemed to be an exceptional level of confusion in relation to police contributions. For example, in one ACPC the reason given for there being no contribution to the joint budget by the police was said to be that they are not able to contribute to budgets over which they have no control. However, in another area there definitely was a contribution made by the police to the budget. In other areas distinctions were made between contributions in services and facilities as opposed to cash contributions, (for example, furnishing video suites, supplying interviewing equipment). The police were often regarded as having made a substantial contribution 'in kind' in this sort of way.

Securing budgets is clearly not easy. In one ACPC on two previous occasions attempts had been made to establish a budget which had been unsuccessful. In another area, one respondent whom we interviewed was extremely resistant to the consideration of a contribution from health agencies to an ACPC budget, giving as a reason the absence of clarity over important budgetary issues, such as how funds would be raised, how they would be used and how they would be monitored. We also found that there were different views on whether providing an ACPC budget was necessary.

In only two of the eight ACPCs, then, did there appear to have been a successful agreement to have an ACPC budget shared evenly between the main agencies, and in these two the scale of that budget was very different. In one of these two cases, where the budget was relatively large, there had been difficulties in collecting the contributions from agencies. In the other case the budget is a very small one for training, and the committee is seeking Welsh Office funding for a research post in order to support the interagency work which it has agreed it should be doing but for which it is unable to find the resources from within its own constituent agencies. In one other ACPC there had been agreement in principle to have a budget, but it had been harder to agree on how to establish fair shares. For this ACPC, the development of a substantial budget formed part of a strategy for the development of an executive role for the ACPC, within which the ACPC was intended to act as the commissioning body for all child protection services. The process was planned to begin with an audit of all child protection services by all agencies, which would include an assessment of the associated costs.

We found that finances had been a particular source difficulty in relation to ACPCs carrying out their responsibility for arranging training. Some agencies appeared to consider that all the costs of training in child protection should be borne by the social services department, who received the Training Support Programme funds. Social services representatives however, tended not to agree with this view.

Even if agencies are not asked to contribute to a general ACPC budget, another financial contribution which is frequently demanded of them is that they should purchase copies of the local procedures booklet for their staff. In at least one instance this caused difficulties in respect of the supply of these handbooks to the area's general practitioners. The FHSA were unwilling to pay for this on the grounds that they do not 'employ' general practitioners. General practitioners were therefore asked if they would buy their own handbook. Eventually a pragmatic solution was found to ensure that all surgeries had a copy of the local procedures handbook.

Examples such as these show how difficulties associated with finances can contribute to barriers between agencies, and can perhaps even on occasion undermine potentially good relationships. We are particularly concerned about the efficiency of systems for distributing information about child protection policy and procedures that depend on agencies purchasing copies of essential documents for their staff. In general we are compelled to conclude that the system of joint financing in its present form simply does not work. It is highly unlikely that the problems involved in creating budgets will go away unless they are addressed differently. In fact, in the present financial climate these problems are likely to become worse rather than better.

Beyond this, it may be salutary to consider what Area Child Protection Committees could potentially do if they had properly established sources of funding. Their ability to develop consistent programmes of training and even of research, if only to ensure that they were able to make full use of the information which they already collect, could be considerably enhanced. Secure and adequate funding could make possible the appointment of a committee secretariat, which might avoid some of the difficulties associated with social services' role as lead agency. One of the Welsh committees has produced a job description for a professional assistant to undertake research and prepare reports for the ACPC. The move has come from frustration at the inability of existing agency staff to do all the work that they can see needs to be done to monitor and improve the effectiveness of interagency work. It is hoped that the post can be jointly funded with some help from the Welsh Office Training Support Programme. In our view this is just one example of the work that could be done, and needs to be done, if agencies are to build on the progress that has been made in recent years.

However, secure and adequate funding could probably only be achieved if central government were to supply it either directly or by dedicating part of each agency's central allocation for this purpose. If government is serious about supporting a positive interagency approach to child protection, it seems reasonable to suggest that this is one way to demonstrate it.

Executive authority

Associated with the question of finance is the wider issue of what is, or ought to be, the authority of the ACPC. Several of our respondents suggested to us that the ACPC would not be truly effective until it had real executive authority over constituent agencies. This echoes the observation of Williams (1992), who distinguishes between a multi- agency approach and an inter- agency approach:

> There is a considerable difference between agencies contributing individually to work with a child and family and those same agencies working together to promote the child's welfare... Working Together provides a model which promotes a multi- rather than an inter- agency approach. Whereas the main tasks of the ACPC raise important issues of interagency work, its composition is rooted in the multi-agency approach. Thus, Working Together regards ACPC members as accountable to the agencies which they represent. It is questionable whether a representative body of this kind is the most effective way of developing policies and procedures which are independent of individual agency perspectives

It might be argued that to give executive authority to the ACPC, especially if combined with some of the changes we have suggested such as established budgets and a secretariat, could risk setting up the ACPC as an agency in its own right and thereby undermining the collaborative approach to child protection. We have some sympathy with this argument. The collaborative approach has a great deal to recommend it, not least in that it creates a permanent expectation that all agencies working with children will carry a sense of responsibility for protecting children from harm. It should not be undermined; on the other hand, it does need to be supported. On balance therefore we would favour strengthening the ACPC by giving it a guaranteed budget and enabling it to employ staff, but at the same time we would not favour giving it the authority to command constituent agencies.

Quality control

One important function of the Area Child Protection Committee is to monitor the conduct and practice of interagency work to protect children in its area. This can include the scrutiny of individual cases where something appears to have gone wrong (as undertaken for example in Part 8 Reviews), the examination of a sample of representative cases, and the use of aggregated case data in order to enable the agencies represented on the committee to reflect on their work.

One of the objectives of our research was to look at the mechanisms that the ACPCs and their constituent agencies had for monitoring practice in order to achieve a high-quality child protection service. We thought it was sensible to ask committee Chairs about local practice in this respect. We therefore asked each Chair three questions:

1) How does the ACPC monitor the impact of its policy on practice?
2) How do agencies monitor the impact of ACPC policies within their organisations?
3) Is there any system of randomly selecting cases for audit?

In view of the information that had been given to us during interviews which suggested increasing trends towards putting registers on to computers, monitoring enquiries to registers, developing sophisticated management information systems, the responses to these questions were surprising. In general we found little evidence, from the Chairs' answers, to confirm the existence of any formal quality control systems. Nor, it has to be said, did we find a great deal of interest in developing such systems. One Chair even went so far as to say 'I wouldn't recognise quality control if it poked me in the eye', although this was certainly an exceptional response.

The Chairs to whom we spoke seemed generally unaware of what monitoring systems existed within individual agencies. This may be because these are also not well developed. However, we knew that in at least one ACPC a constituent agency (from health) was putting forward its own internal quality control process as the basis for the development of an interagency quality system.

Overall, the picture is of what one respondent described as 'a somewhat relaxed approach' to monitoring and quality control processes. We were disappointed at this. It seems to us that monitoring the quality of services is an essential part of the Area Child Protection Committees' remit, and this cannot be done only by examining cases where problems have become evident. Mills and Vine (1990) for example, drawing on a 'critical incident reporting' model derived from aviation and anaesthesia practice, propose that non-fatal cases should be examined as well as fatal ones:

> Central to the 'critical incident' approach is the acceptance that errors committed by individuals and agencies should be reported irrespective of outcome ... It is therefore proposed that case review working groups are established by Area Child Protection Committees with a mandate to review on a regular basis critical, as well as fatal, incidents.

To some extent this is happening. District committees and subcommittees are in many areas looking at cases in an effort to monitor and improve practice. Usually this is initiated by individuals raising particular cases, often because something appears to have gone wrong. One or two areas did appear to have some random sampling of cases for audit. Most, however, did not. However, we were encouraged by the current emphasis on the development of more sophisticated management information systems, which may in the future lend themselves to this kind of analysis. This represents a significant improvement in many areas. One representative described the statistics previously available to the ACPC as 'worse than useless'.

In another ACPC area we were impressed with the fact that referral rates were being monitored as well as, and alongside, figures for registration and deregistration. Too often in the past registration levels have been used as indicators of the incidence of child abuse upon which to base resource allocation, despite general awareness of the vagaries of the registration process. Giller et al. (1992), and Gibbons et al. (1993) have both identified problems with the criteria adopted by authorities for registration. In fact Giller et al. concluded that there was little qualitative difference between those children who drop out of the child protection system at one of the filters along the way, and those who do not.

It is also the case that registration figures change over time because of factors that may be unrelated to the incidence of child abuse, (for example, government guidance and the changing understanding of the purpose for which registers should be used). It is noteworthy that in the 1980s the trend throughout the U.K., and within Wales was for increasing numbers of children to be registered each year. For the last few years, however, registration levels within Wales have been declining. One authority claims on the basis of figures not yet available to have nearly halved the registration numbers over the past 18 months.

Summary

Chapter 5 began by looking at the effectiveness of the ACPC meetings. In general there was a view that agencies had come a long way towards overcoming interagency barriers and that there was a lot of good will, although this was not invariably the case. Meetings were generally considered to have enough time to consider issues and to be handled very effectively in terms of advance notice of issues and the process of chairing. By focusing on the chairs of the ACPCs we were able to explore the process of policy development within ACPCs (using parental participation in child protection conferences as a case in point), and to look at policy that had been developed as well as policy areas where little progress had so far been made despite the Chair's interest.

We then looked at the balance in Area Child Protection Committee policy between the three areas of investigation, prevention and treatment. We found that according to almost all members the overwhelming emphasis was on investigation, with particularly little consideration being given to treatment. Agencies also appear to be differentially involved in the management process of ACPCs; this may be related to the imbalance in policy mentioned above, as well as to the relative fragmentation of some constituent agencies as a result of major reorganisations.

We saw how ACPCs attempt to increase the effectiveness of their operations by the use of both functional subcommittees and geographical district committees. We explored the issues of financial support for ACPCs and the question whether they should have executive authority. We concluded that having a budget would probably increase the effectiveness of ACPC operations, but that executive authority might bring more problems than benefits. Finally, we reviewed the extent to which ACPCs have established mechanisms of quality control.

6 Interagency procedures

In Chapter 3 we discussed the reliance of agencies on written material as one of the means of ensuring that practice was consistent with child protection policy. Two forms of written material were mentioned. Firstly, there are internal procedures documents which vary from agency to agency and from area to area. Although these are relatively common in certain agencies such as social services departments, they are by no means universal. For the police, standing orders or their equivalent are virtually universal. Secondly, there are interagency procedures developed by the Area Child Protection Committees. These are sometimes referred to as 'manuals', and as previously noted a distinction may be made between manuals and handbooks, both being produced in the same ACPC region to reflect a difference between the type of information that all professionals need to know and the type needed only by professionals more intensively involved in child protection work.

For a number of reasons local procedures handbooks are extremely important documents in the management of child protection. Firstly, they produce a degree of agreement and consistency across agencies on the procedures that are expected to be followed in cases of a child being abused. Secondly, they may serve to highlight potential and actual areas of disagreement between agencies, which can then be addressed. Thirdly, they are a tool for ensuring that practice adheres to policy, (both for central government to be satisfied that local policy reflects government policy, and for the ACPC to be satisfied that local practice operates within the policy established by that Committee). Finally, they serve as a vehicle through which agencies are able to develop better working relationships at the level of senior management. For these reasons, and because the Welsh Office review provided the authors with an opportunity to examine a number of these documents in detail, making comparisons across ACPCs, these written guidelines will be explored in some depth.

Working Together (paragraphs 2.18 - 2.19, Appendix 6) offers considerable guidance on the nature, purpose and content of the handbooks. They should be concerned with interagency processes rather than with detailed professional practice, should be revised regularly, and should be available to all members of staff, the public (through libraries), and independent practitioners concerned with children and families (including independent schools, day care centres and local voluntary organisations). It is recommended that they should follow a standardised format of:

- Law and Definitions
- Who is Involved
- Referral and Recognition
- Immediate Protection and Planning the Investigation
- Investigation and Initial Assessment
- Child Protection Conference and Decision Making about the Need for Registration
- Comprehensive Child Protection Assessment and Planning
- Implementation, Review and De-registration
- Other
- Local Agency Procedures

As to layout, the guidance recommends an indexed loose-leaf format, which should be easy to read (that is, having concise wording and good typography).

For many Area Child Protection Committee members, the handbook represents the end-product of a considerable amount of ACPC work. As such it reflects the effective operation of the ACPC and the motivation, enthusiasm, and particular interests of its members. Representatives will probably consider it necessary to take it back to their agencies for approval before being able to commit them to it. In case of particularly controversial issues such as that of abuse by professionals, negotiations may be required and even face to face meetings between senior managers of the different agencies, before material can be agreed for inclusion.

In recent years the handbooks have had to be rewritten, or at least substantially revised, quite frequently. It is likely that most authorities will have felt the need for significant changes in the handbooks following the Beckford Inquiry (London Borough of Brent and Brent Health Authority, 1985) and the Cleveland Inquiry (Butler-Sloss, 1988). Following the implementation of the Children Act 1989 in October 1991, the changes were so fundamental that ACPCs were required to start more or less from scratch and to re-develop their entire handbooks. Now that the government has indicated its intention to reissue *Working Together* to take into account the research findings in twenty commissioned pieces of research in child protection (Department of Health, 1995) and the need for a 'refocusing', it seems likely that the local procedures manuals will again need to be revised.

Although social services has the lead role in the development of the handbook, because of the work involved by all members (usually through a policy and procedures subcommittee), representatives of other agencies take considerable pride in the achievement. Moreover, the process of designing the handbook appears to serve a dual purpose: not only is it important to create a final product which will promote the best interagency practice in child protection, but also the production of the handbook is often the vehicle through which agencies work together at a managerial and policy-making level to promote generally better interagency working relations. This has potential benefits for smooth working relations between practitioners.

Local procedures handbooks and the Welsh Office review

Because of their significant role in translating child protection policy into child protection practice, an analysis of the handbooks featured prominently in our research for the Welsh Office. We began with an overview of handbooks followed by a scrutiny of particular subject areas. Subject areas were evaluated by observing both how fully the issue was covered in the handbook, and how closely the material in the handbooks adhered to government guidance.

Twenty individual subject areas were selected for closer scrutiny (the numbers in brackets indicate the relevant paragraphs in *Working Together*):

1) *What the public should do if concerned (2.18; 4.47; Appendix 6, Section III)*

2) *What various agencies should do if concerned (Part 4, Appendix 6, Section III)*

3) *Criteria for joint investigation by police and social workers (4.17, 5.13.1)*

4) *Where no substance is revealed to the cause for concern (5.14.10)*

5) *Written reports required for case conferences (6.33)*

6) *Requirements for registration (6.39)*

7) *Criteria for deregistration (6.43-6.46)*

8) *Involvement of parents in child protection investigation (1.4-1.8 and 5.8)*

9) *Involvement of parents in case conferences (6.11, 6.14)*

10) *Involvement of children in child protection process (1.4-1.8, 5.8, 5.14.7)*

11) *Involvement of children in case conferences (6.13-6.14)*

12) *Case conference exclusion criteria (6.14-6.17)*

13) *Core groups, function and composition (6.26; Appendix 4: Part III)*

14) *Appeals against registration or deregistration decisions, and complaints (6.21)*

15) *Abuse by professionals (5.14.2, 5.19-5.20, 5.22.2, Appendix 6: Section IX)*

16) *Organised abuse (5.26, Appendix 6: Section IX)*

17) *Young people as abusers (5.24)*

18) *Female genital mutilation (3.9, Appendix 6: Section IX)*

19) *Media policy (5.26.8)*

20) *Ethnicity, culture and language (including Welsh language) issues*

These topics were chosen not only because they addressed important issues but also because they appeared to offer scope for diversity. For fullness of coverage, subject areas were rated as follows:

0	1	2	3	4
Not covered at all	Mentioned, or refer to *Working Together* only	Covered briefly	Covered substantially, but not in depth	Covered in depth, fully, and comprehensively

These ratings were then aggregated to provide an item-by-item analysis and an overview. A summary of the handbooks is provided in table 6.1.

Table 6.1
Eight ACPC local procedures handbooks

ACPC Handbook	Sections (including Appendix)	Pages
ACPC A		
Manual	8	75
Handbook	11	150
ACPC B	8	80
ACPC C	8	167
ACPC D	10	56
ACPC E		
English	5	113
Welsh	5	113
ACPC F	7	163
ACPC G	8	225
ACPC H	14	152

All handbooks followed a format that was broadly based on the guidance in Appendix 6 of *Working Together*. Some handbooks used all the headings suggested by *Working Together*, while others used fewer and amalgamated some of the *Working Together* headings. Apart from one bound A4 booklet, all had a looseleaf format. Most were well presented and printed. The layout was generally accessible to the reader. Only one was indexed but all included a table of contents of varying degrees of detail. Surprisingly in Wales, only one of the eight ACPCs had produced a bilingual (Welsh) language edition, although a second ACPC was planning one. There is substantial variation in size of handbooks, the largest being nearly four times the size of the smallest.

Overview of the twenty subject areas

In general, the content of material that was contained in the handbooks departed very little from the guidance in *Working Together*. There was however, much variation in the fullness of the coverage of a wide range of issues, a number being completely omitted and others treated in a cursory manner. The most telling feature is the complete omission of certain subjects. There were a large number of these; larger than we expected. From the potential coverage of 20 subjects across eight ACPCs (total 168) there were 19 '0' ratings, indicating that nearly one eighth (11.3%) of the issues that we looked at were not covered at all in those handbooks. For those issues rated either 0 or 1 the number rises to 41 (24.4%), indicating that for a quarter of the topics, the issues are either not addressed in guidance at all, or are addressed so briefly as to be unlikely to provide a guide for interagency practice; that is, practitioners would be unlikely to know what to do because of a lack of guidance.

It is also useful to look at which particular topics get most fully covered and which least. The five most fully covered issues were:

Requirements for registration (32)
Children's involvement in conferences (27)
Criteria for deregistration (27)
What agencies should do (26)
Core groups, their function and composition (25)

(Only one issue received the highest possible score of 32, where all eight handbooks received a rating of 4.) It may be thought reassuring that the requirements for registration and criteria for deregistration are so well covered. A surprising finding is that child involvement in case conferences comes out higher than that of parents (not included in the five), especially since the content of the handbooks suggested that agencies allow themselves more discretion as regards the attendance of children at conferences. It may be, of course, that it is precisely because of this increased discretion that fuller guidance is found to be needed.

The five least well covered issues are:

Appeals and complaints (18)
Written reports for conferences (16)
Media policy (14)
Criteria for joint investigation (14)
Female genital mutilation (6)

The exceptionally low rating of female genital mutilation is due to the fact that three-quarters of the handbooks did not include it at all as a topic area. Criteria for joint investigation may be a matter that agencies prefer to decide at strategy discussions, on a case by case basis, as long as no particular problems arise. Nevertheless, its inclusion among the five least well-covered issues is surprising because of the heavy emphasis put on investigation within ACPC priorities. In relation to complaints and appeals, it may be that some ACPCs assume that the within-agency mechanisms for dealing with complaints (for example those under section 26 of the Children Act 1989) will be sufficient. A similar factor may apply to written reports. The low rating here is because of the lack of detail, even though all handbooks address it to some extent. It may be that agencies only expect social workers to prepare written reports, and detail concerning these reports may be highlighted in places other than the local procedures handbook (for example, within social services procedures manuals where these exist). Media policy appears to be seen by ACPCs as an issue of limited relevance, although as we argue later this is a short-sighted attitude.

In addition to how fully material is covered, there were also variations in the nature of the guidance given. For example, it could be noted that there was substantial variation in advice to different agencies about what to do when concerned about the welfare of a child. It is notable that no two handbooks gave the same advice about what general practitioners should do if they suspect abuse.

The uneven coverage of topics may reflect a number of factors, including a lack of perceived urgency of the issue for the agency - for instance female genital mutilation is only likely to be a pressing concern in areas with a particular ethnic population; the concerted effort to resolve certain difficult issues by one or two agencies but not necessarily by others - for instance in relation to abuse by professionals; and the sheer difficulty of resolving certain controversial issues - such as general practitioner referrals. However, one implication of this uneven coverage in guidance is that practitioners may be operating in a policy vacuum in relation to some of the most difficult - or most important - decisions.

Detailed account of the twenty subject areas

For each topic heading, a synopsis of government guidance is followed by a discussion of the degree to which the topic is addressed by the various handbooks and their conformity with guidance.

1) What the public should do if they become concerned. (2.18, 4.47; Appendix 6, Section III)

Working Together says that the handbooks should be made available to the public (for example through libraries) and should be written in such a way as to help members of the public to know what to do if they have concerns. It also emphasises that they may need to be reassured about confidentiality.

There was much variation in how this material was incorporated into the handbooks. In one handbook, there was no mention of what members of the public should do if they are concerned. In most the advice for members of the public was buried away in the middle of the handbook, rather than being immediately accessible. In these cases it appeared to be more in the nature of a statement to professionals about the public than a message to the public about what to do. In some cases the material on who to contact was close to the list of phone numbers to contact; in others they were in separate sections. All handbooks did include a list of relevant addresses and phone numbers.

2) What various agencies should do if they become concerned. (Part 4, Appendix 6, Section III)

This section is a message to various professionals about their responsibilities in child protection. We looked both at the overall pattern and the advice given to a particular professional group for purposes of comparison between handbooks. *Working Together* sets out the roles of various agencies and how their 'duties and functions should be organised in order to contribute to inter-agency cooperation for the protection of children' (4.1). It continues: 'The responsibility for protecting children should not fall entirely to one agency: awareness and appreciation of another agency's role will contribute greatly to collaborative practices.' The role of the handbook in ensuring mutual awareness of child protection functions is obviously seen as being very important.

Six of the eight handbooks included comprehensive information on the roles of the various agencies. These sections ordinarily took up a major proportion of the handbook. Of the two that did not include substantial information, one addressed the roles of various agencies very briefly, and the other not at all. We decided to look in particular at the advice for general practitioners. The *Working Together* guidance indicates that when a general practitioner is concerned that a child may be, or is, the subject of abuse, that information should be shared with the statutory agencies. All except one of the handbooks incorporated guidance for general practitioners. Since the relationship of general practitioners to the child protection system is in itself problematic (both for the organisational reasons discussed in previous chapters and because of issues to do with confidential relationships with patients), it is not surprising that there should be some diversity in the advice given to this group in the handbooks. Of the seven handbooks that offered advice to general practitioners, no two mechanisms for referring concerns were identical, despite all being loosely based on the guidance in *Working Together*. The differences largely come from applying different procedures to different situations. In one handbook, there is a different/additional procedure for sexual abuse from that for other forms of abuse. In another handbook, there are four circumstances described, (emergency, non-emergency, sexual abuse, and worrying background), all of which have a different set of requirements for the general practitioner. In some cases the general practitioner is advised to refer to the social services department at the same time as referring to the paediatrician. In others, the referral to the paediatrician can come before, (as a consultation), or even instead, (passing to the paediatrician the responsibility to make the referral).

Considering that different sections of the different ACPC handbooks are often similar to the extent of using identical wording, leaving aside verbatim extracts from *Working Together*, it seems reasonable to conclude that this variation reflects the results of different locally negotiated agreements. It is more difficult to determine the extent to which these divergent solutions are manifestations of communication difficulties and unresolved issues between general practitioners and Area Child Protection Committees. For example, the ACPC producing the handbook which contains no reference to general practitioners was known to have experienced other difficulties in its relationships with this group of professionals.

3) Criteria for joint investigation by police and social workers. (4.17, 5.13.1)

The original momentum for joint investigation by police and social workers came from the Bexley experiment (Metropolitan Police and London Borough of Bexley, 1987), which was largely concerned with coordinating intervention in cases of suspected sexual abuse. The scheme was considered to be successful, and by 1990 joint investigation (of sexual abuse at least) had become established as the norm (Community Care, 1990).

Not all investigations proceed in the same way, and at early stages decisions have to be made about which agency should take the more active or even exclusive role. A strategy discussion, which need not necessarily be a meeting, should 'plan the investigation and in particular the role of each agency and the extent of joint investigation' (*Working Together*, para 5.13.1). Some situations may not require the application of interagency procedures for the purposes of investigation beyond the initial consultation between police and social services; for example the suspected abuse of a child by a stranger where there is no question of parental complicity or negligence (*Working Together*, para 5.23), which is likely to be pursued by the police acting alone. There may be other examples where after the initial consultation between the two agencies the investigation will be undertaken by social services, without the police playing a role.

Brown and Fuller (1991) describe the practice of 'joint interviewing on a selective basis only.' They suggest that 'differences can lie in the type of abuse which is included, the extent to which investigators (whether police or social workers) specialise in child protection work, the proportion and type of case subject to joint procedures, and the point at which both the police and social workers cease to be involved in the case'.

Our examination of the handbooks was intended to discover to what extent they incorporated criteria or guidelines that might help the police and social services to decide how far an investigation should be a joint one. We found that all ACPCs apparently consider themselves to be operating a joint investigation policy, at least to the extent that all investigations are jointly planned. However, it was also clear that only a few have given consideration to the question of what types of situations will warrant joint investigation beyond the initial planning stage, leaving the matter to be decided on a case by case basis. This may be satisfactory. It can only be assumed that the basis for the decision lies within the understanding of the agencies' remit and the responsibilities of those individuals undertaking the discussion and subsequent decision.

The handbooks indicate that in some cases social services may, after the initial consultation, undertake the investigation alone, and that in some cases the police may do so. One ACPC distinguishes those investigations that will be undertaken by social services alone - physical abuse which has not resulted in significant harm, and neglect not severe enough to warrant joint investigation - from those which will be joint. The latter include serious physical abuse, sexual abuse, significant harm resulting from neglect, and severe emotional abuse. Another ACPC indicated that all sexual abuse cases will be jointly investigated, presumably leaving other cases to be decided on a case by case basis.

These differences highlight significant variations between ACPCs on what matters will be jointly investigated. Generally, whether further variations exist within an ACPC area may depend on the extent to which ACPC policy is explicit on this topic. Our findings suggest that only one local procedures handbook had a level of specificity that would be sufficient to guide interagency practice.

4) Where no substance is revealed to the cause for concern. (5.14.10)

The essential elements of the *Working Together* guidance are that the lack of substantiation should be communicated in writing to the relevant people, acknowledging the distress; drawing attention to the investigation duty of the agency, and offering support, if necessary from alternative sources.

Six of the eight handbooks addressed this issue. Of the six, five were very close to the *Working Together* guidance; one had some minor differences and one did not refer to alternative sources of counselling. Overall, this seemed to be a relatively straightforward matter for ACPCs, without many of the controversial overtones raised by some of the other issues. It is surprising therefore that two agencies should decide not to include it. One can only presume that in those areas, when such issues arise, practitioners will be dealing with situations in an absence of guidance.

5) Written reports for case conferences. (6.33)

The guidance in *Working Together* advises that all participants should prepare for conferences, but that in addition to this investigating officers and key workers should prepare reports on past and present incidents of abuse, on family circumstances, on the work undertaken and on proposals for the future. Other professionals should also bring relevant reports (for example police statements, school reports, medical reports including growth charts). These should be treated as confidential.

Only two handbooks had substantial guidance on this issue. No handbook omitted the topic completely, indicating that in all areas there would be some expectation that reports would be prepared. However, very few supplied details on who should prepare what kinds of reports, what they should cover or how they should be used.

6) Requirements for registration. (6.39)

These are not the same as categories for registration (neglect, physical injury, sexual abuse or emotional abuse) although the two are occasionally confused. Requirements for registration provide guidance for agencies on the kinds of situations that should result in a child's name being added to the child protection register. The guidance emphasises signficant harm and the need for a child protection plan as the basis for registration. Significant harm can be established either on the basis of identifiable incidents (including omission as well as commission) or the expectation of significant harm. Registration requirements are important because a clear judicious use of the child protection register will enable it to function as a useful tool in child protection both for the purposes of protecting individual children and for service planning and development. An injudicious tendency towards over-registration can result in agencies becoming bogged down in the system requirements of large numbers on the register, which can ultimately undermine the ability to protect children. As observed by Corpe (1987), 'In extending the net too far, we run the risk of numbing our senses to the cases to which we should be alerted' (p.24). Concepts of 'net-widening' and 'threshold lowering' in child protection are currently being critically examined, and 'filtering' stages, including registration, have featured in a number of recent government commissioned research studies, (e.g. Giller et al, 1992; Gibbons et al, 1993). ACPC members considered the local procedures handbook as the major influence on decision-making at case conferences. A large number mentioned training, and several referred to distinct agency perspectives, for instance that the police were more likely than other agencies to favour registration. In general (with only two exceptions) there appeared to be no additional guidance on registration criteria other than what was in the local procedures handbooks, which in turn closely followed the guidance in *Working Together*. Other ACPC members suggested that staff understanding of registration policy came from the case conference process itself, that is, from the chair or the social worker at the conference.

On this issue there was least variation between ACPCs. All eight handbooks had incorporated *verbatim* section 6.39 from *Working Together* as a basis for the decision on when to register children. In view of the tendency toward an over-cautious use of the register advocated by some ('If in doubt, register'), this clarity of agreed interagency policy on the use of the register should help to keep the registration practice focused. One ACPC member described how the impulse of some case conference participants to register too readily had on occasion been controlled by simply reading out the criteria from the handbook.

7) Criteria for deregistration. (6.43-6.46)

Working Together describes four groups of reasons why children may be deregistered.

These are that the original factors which led to registration no longer apply, that the child and family have moved permanently to another area, that the child is no longer a child in the eyes of the law (becomes 18 or gets married), or that the child dies. The first of these will always require a conference. For deregistration to occur *all* members of the review conference must agree that the risk of abuse is no longer there or is no longer of a level to warrant registration. In addition to looking at how fully the handbooks addressed this issue, we therefore asked in each case if the handbook was explicit that *all* members were required to agree. We looked for any suggestions about how disagreements should be treated.

All handbooks dealt adequately with the area of deregistration except for one - and even that did specify the reasons for removal from the register - and included case conference requirements for the first group of reasons. All handbooks, except one, referred to the four groups of reasons for deregistration, although one did not specify that a conference was required for the first category only. Five handbooks did specify, in line with the *Working Together* guidance, that the decision must be unanimous, but three did not. One actually said that all those 'working with the child and family' must decide, which is different from the formulation in *Working Together*). On the point of handling dissent one had no policy at all, and another did not appear to address it directly. The remainder found different ways to deal with disagreement. For several the preferred method was to maintain the status quo until the following review, when if there had been no new evidence of risk, and members were still unable to agree, the chair would make the decision. One handbook referred the decision upwards to the District Child Protection Committee. For another, the disagreement would simply be recorded, although the subsequent action regarding deregistration was unclear.

8) Involvement of parents in child protection investigation. (1.4-1.8, 5.8 and 6.11)

The guidance in *Working Together* is emphatic about involving children and parents in the child protection process, and builds on those provisions of the Children Act 1989 which stress the participation of children and parents. If parents are to be meaningfully involved in child protection conferences, then the groundwork for participation in the process must be established long before they get to the conference. *Working Together* says: '...involvement of child and adults in child protection conferences will not be effective unless they are fully involved from the outset in all stages of the child protection process, and unless from the time of referral there is as much openness and honesty as possible between families and professionals' (6.11). This has been further supported by the government publication, *The Challenge of Partnership in Child Protection: Practice Guide* (Department of Health/Social Services Inspectorate, 1995).

This issue appeared to polarise the handbooks more than most others. Three of the eight were extremely full and detailed, not only stating the principles of involving parents at this stage, but also describing the means by which to translate the principles into practice. One had a policy which was particularly strong on guiding attitudes and practice. On the other hand, three handbooks did not address the issue at all, or addressed it so briefly as to be tokenistic.

9) Involvement of parents in case conferences. (6.11, 6.14)

The *Working Together* guidance is again explicit on this issue: 'It is important that ACPCs should formally agree the principle of including parents and children in all conferences. Guidance on their inclusion must be contained in the local child protection procedures' (6.14). Because of the importance of this principle, the key statements within the eight local handbooks are reproduced here in full.

They (parents/carers) should be invited to attend for all or part of the conference unless in the view of the Chairperson of the conference, their presence will preclude a full and proper consideration of the child's interests.

Parents and children must be informed of child protection conferences and invited to attend for all of the conference unless, exceptionally, in the view of the chair of the conference, their presence will preclude a full and proper consideration of the child's interests.

There should be an assumption that parents/carers will attend...

Parents will normally have the opportunity to attend and participate as fully as is practicable in all initial and subsequent review Child Protection Conferences...

Parents must be invited to attend all Case Conferences, unless it is felt that their presence will preclude a full and proper consideration of the child's best interests.

The purposes of the Conference will be hindered if parents or carers are not present throughout Child Protection Conferences.

Parents must be ... invited to attend but the timing of their attendance needs to be discussed... On initial case conferences - difficult for the best interests of the child to remain the objective focus of the Conference if the parents are present throughout. Parents may be invited to attend the whole of a follow-up Case Conference.

The parents, or others who have parental responsibility, must be invited to attend if this is consistent with safeguarding and promoting the welfare of the child.

It can be seen that all eight ACPCs have a statement addressing the policy on parental participation at case conferences, but the detail - and even the principle - varies greatly. In some there is further material on how to facilitate participation, how to prepare parents for attendance and how to support parents during and after the conference. In others there is little more than the statement, and in others this statement is qualified to the point where in some areas there appears to be a presumption of non-participation instead of a presumption of participation. Considering what a major change in practice was represented by the introduction of parental participation, and the degree of official pressure which lay behind it, it is disconcerting to find such a degree of variation in the policy expressed in the handbooks. Most ACPCs fully support the policy and are clearly committed to it. Their handbooks spell out why parental involvement in case conferences is a good thing, and more importantly, the steps that can be taken to implement it. However, others qualify the policy so heavily that it would be hardly surprising if practitioners believed that behind the statement requiring it, there was little support at policy level.

10) Involvement of children in child protection processes. (1.4-1.8, 5.8, 5.14.7)

Working Together refers to information being given to children, including leaflets for older children, seeking the views of children, and to the importance of keeping the needs of the child as the focus of all enquiries, working at the child's pace, and using language that the child can understand.

Although all of the handbooks make some mention of involving children in the process, there are significant variations, for example, in the attention given to children's views and wishes during investigation. In some the issue was only mentioned in conjunction either with the views of parents, or as part of the context of attending case conferences. In others, however, the practice implications helpfully go beyond the guidance in *Working Together*.

11) Involvement of children in case conferences. (6.13-6.14)

Because this is such an important issue, we again quote the key statements from each handbook.

> Parents *and children* must be informed of child protection conferences and invited to attend for all of the conference unless, exceptionally, in the view of the chair of the conference, their presence will preclude a full and proper consideration of the child's interests. (our italics)

> Whenever children have sufficient understanding and are able to express their wishes and feelings and to participate in the process of investigation, assessment, planning and review, they should be encouraged to attend conferences.

> Consideration must be given to inviting a child to a Child Protection Conference, particularly when children are old enough to express their wishes and feelings and to participate in the process of assessment, planning and review.

> Some thought needs to be given to the involvement of children within the context of their age and understanding... Much depends on the maturity and understanding of the child. Many young people/teenagers could attend given the right support, unless the usual reasons for exclusion apply.

> Consideration should also be given to inviting a child, who is of a sufficient age and understanding, to participate. It will be a matter for professional judgment in each situation to decide whether attendance would be in the child's best interest. (This statement is used by two ACPCs.)

...where the child has sufficient understanding, are able to express their views and feelings and can participate, they have a right to attend.

The child if of sufficient age and understanding must be invited to attend the whole or part of the conference. The child's attendance must be consistent with promoting and safeguarding their welfare.

In accordance with the guidance in 6.14, all ACPCs addressed the issue, although in varying depth. This section highlights most clearly how subtle nuances of language can be used to convey a message different from that contained in guidance. Clearly the reliance on the test of the child's being of sufficient age and understanding is a necessary precondition. But the phrases 'promoting and safeguarding their welfare', and 'the child's best interests', whilst undeniably sound, allow considerable leeway for discretionary judgements which may be based more on professional misgivings than on objective reasons. It is interesting that only one handbook refers to the child's *right* to attend.

12) Case conference exclusion criteria. (6.14-6.17)

There are times when parents should not be included. The essential elements of the guidance on exclusion are that it should be kept to a minimum, that procedures should lay down criteria for exclusion (with examples cited), and that prosecution for an offence does not justify exclusion. The decision to exclude should rest with the chair and should be recorded. The guidance is directed at whole- or part- time exclusion, and at the exclusion of the child as well as the parent(s) or carer(s).

All handbooks contain some indication of the basis on which to exclude parents from attending child protection conferences. Few, however, are clear about distinguishing between parents and children for the purposes of exclusion, most emphasising parents. Some distinguish between criteria for total or partial exclusion, while others do not. The criteria vary significantly in degree of explicitness and detail. The most explicit guidance included seven criteria, four for exclusion from the whole of the conference, three for exclusion from part of the conference. The least explicit only gave one basis for both whole- and part- exclusion. One ACPC, as described above, appeared to assume that at least partial exclusion would be the norm for all initial case conferences.

One issue highlighting a departure from the guidance is the question of legal proceedings (prosecution for an offence) being a basis for exclusion. Most felt that this would be a basis for at least partial exclusion, on the grounds that the police might hear material that could be construed as evidence, or the local authority legal advisor giving advice to the conference. Two handbooks make no mention of legal or police issues, and a third describes a system of the chairperson administering a caution to parents about the potential use in evidence of statements made in the conference. The extent of variation from official guidance on this matter suggests a need to make the guidance to agencies fuller or more explicit.

13) Core groups, their function and composition. (6.26; Appendix 4: Part III)

Core groups are described in *Working Together* (6.26) as 'a group led by the key worker (which) has been identified to work with the family'. There is no requirement in guidance to have core groups although details of their composition are meant to be included on the register details. *Working Together* actually says very little about them, which may be because it was drafted at a time when the concept was being developed. They are still a fairly recent practice trend. Core groups are also referred to in the standards set out in *Inspecting for Quality: Evaluating Performance in Child Protection*, (Social Services Inspectorate/Department of Health,1993), for example in relation to decisions at case conferences (standard 5), implementing child protection plans (standard 8) and reviewing child protection plans (standard 9).

It was found that all eight ACPCs advised the use of core groups, and six were extremely clear about the purpose and function of the groups and the criteria for membership - that is, a close working relationship with the child and family. The lack of clarity in two cases is noticeable, especially as in those two the issue of child and parent membership is not addressed. In only one of the other six, where core groups were clearly defined, was the family not seen as part of the core group, and we understood this to be intentional. It is interesting to compare this relative emphasis on core groups with the finding of Colton, Roberts and Sanders (1996) in looking at Part 8 case reviews that evidence of the use of core groups was only found in three of the six cases where children's names were on the child protection register (see also chapter 8).

14) Appeals against registration or deregistration decisions, and complaints. (6.21)

The *Working Together* guidance is clear on the distinction between the two different types of dissatisfactions which parents may wish to have addressed, those about the actions of individual agencies and those about a case conference resulting in registration or a decision not to register. It emphasises the importance that 'parents are clear about where the responsibility for decision making lies' (6.21). All agencies who are a part of the child protection process should have their own complaints procedures which parents can use. Additionally, however, there should be a procedure for dealing with complaints about a conference as such, either as a separate procedure, or using the complaints procedure of the lead agency.

There was considerable variation between handbooks in the issues addressed, and the procedures adopted to address them. Only half of the handbooks made reference to the two types of dissatisfaction. Of the remainder, three addressed either agency complaints or conference appeals, but not both, while the fourth made no mention of either. Several agencies had developed elaborate procedures for dealing with appeals against the action of a conference. The outcomes of such appeals were less clear. In several it was implied that the outcome of appeal could be a reversal of the original decision. In others it was stated that the outcome would be a reconsideration of the original decision by a reconvened case conference.

15) Abuse by professionals. (5.14.2, 5.19-5.20, 5.22.2, Appendix 6: Section IX)

Working Together covers this area most substantially in relation to children who are being looked after, either in residential care or foster care, but also includes provisions for dealing with abuse by individuals in contact with children by virtue of their professional role. The need to separate out the three types of process (child protection, disciplinary proceedings and managerial decisions) is made clear, with the emphasis on child protection as the first priority. Colton and Vanstone (1996) in their study of seven men who had sexually abused children in their trust noted the scarcity of literature on this topic. Colton, Roberts and Sanders (1996) noted that two of the 21 part 8 reports they studied concerned men who used their position as teachers to sexually abuse children, (see chapter 8).

The handbooks were examined in relation to abuse by foster carers as an example of professional abuse, because such abuse is known to present special difficulties for agencies (Thomas, 1995). Foster carers are not employees of the agency, nor are they parents like any other parents. Abuse by foster carers, as a separate issue, is also addressed in *Working Together* (paras 5.19.2-5.19.4).

Two of the eight handbooks did not address issues of professional abuse at all. Abuse by foster carers was fully covered in only half of the manuals. It is surprising that the issue of professional abuse in general was addressed in several of those that did not address abuse by foster carers. Of those handbooks dealing with professional abuse, some took pains to be clear about defining terms and specifying to whom the procedures applied (for example in terms of alleged abusers being employees of those agencies which are constituents of the ACPC). The importance of an initial strategy meeting, and in some cases subsequent strategy meetings, was indicated. Some handbooks addressed the difficult and sensitive questions of who is to tell the alleged abuser, who is to tell the parents and the timing of this informing.

16) Organised abuse. (5.26, Appendix 6: Section IX)

Organised abuse is defined in *Working Together* as 'a generic term which covers abuse which may involve a number of abusers, a number of abused children and often encompass different forms of abuse.' The essential features of the guidance provided are the need for ACPC procedures, the timing of interventions, the involvement of senior managers, resource considerations, co-operation across geographical boundaries, and regular strategy meetings. A statement about the need for treatment is also included. Dealing with the media is also highlighted (see below). Organised abuse is something which can arise in any part of the country, at any time, and it seems to be coming to light more and more frequently. As indicated in *Working Together*, it is a phenomenon that crosses boundaries. It would therefore be extremely worrying if agency procedures in relation to this were not sufficiently detailed to guide interagency practice at the point when they are needed. It is, as the Rochdale and Orkney enquiries have illustrated, an area of practice that can leave agencies open to a substantial amount of criticism and arouses intense professional anxiety.

All of the handbooks contained material on organised abuse. In five we thought the issue was adequately covered, including the definition of organised abuse, the question of who to contact, and the composition and functions of strategy meetings. In one case *Working Together* was quoted directly without any reference to local procedures and with two very significant omissions: abuse across geographical boundaries and resource considerations. Only three of the handbooks referred to treatment of children involved in organised abuse. One quoted from *Working Together*, the other two addressed it in respect of potential criminal prosecution. In doing so they hinted at rather different perspectives - on the one hand:

> ... the need to prosecute and the prime importance of the therapeutic needs of any child(ren). The Crown Prosecution Service must form part of any consultation in this regard ...

and on the other:

> ... the treatment of the children involved. Particular thought should be given as to whether any therapy might damage the child's credibility as a witness in a criminal case ...

17) Young abusers.(5.24)

Working Together emphasises that the abuser as well as the victim should be the subject of child protection procedures. It highlights five areas that a child protection conference should address, emphasises the need for a comprehensive assessment (to be followed by a further conference) and stresses the importance of the role of child psychiatrist.

The guidance contained within the handbooks was very diverse. One did not address it at all. Two, by contrast, not only gave the *Working Together* guidance, but also included material from the *Memorandum of Good Practice* and indicators of abuse by young people. In between these two extremes were varying degrees of coverage of the issue. Only three referred to the importance of the role of the child psychiatrist in this area of work. Of those that did not, it was interesting to note that one actually quoted passages from *Working Together* immediately before and after the reference to the role of the child psychiatrist, but omitted that particular section. In most cases it appeared to be understood that child protection procedures should be used for both victims and abusers, although the phrasing used was sometimes unclear.

18) Female genital mutilation.(3.9, Appendix 6: Section IX)

Working Together essentially describes the law, and suggests that the issue should be included in local procedural handbooks.

Only two of the eight handbooks addressed this issue. One included a statement of the law and guidance on when to refer, to whom to refer, and indicated that a strategy discussion ought to be arranged. The other contained a good deal of information on the issue, but very little actual guidance on what to do if a situation should arise. The remaining six handbooks omitted the issue completely. This may be a reflection of cultural bias, with those committees not having policies assuming that it is not relevant to them because of the low numbers in the population likely to be affected by this practice. It may also indicate a lack of appreciation of the need for a positive approach to race and cultural issues within Welsh agencies specifically (although it should be noted that we have not carried out a similar examination of handbooks in England). This question is explored further below.

19) Media Policy

Working Together only gives guidance in handling the media in the context of organised abuse, where it states that 'media management is also a matter which should be covered in ACPC procedures' (5.26.8).

Of the eight handbooks, only two gave anything more than a most cursory treatment of media issues. Of those two, one incorporated it into a policy to deal with other situations such as Part 8 case reviews. Four dealt with media issues in a very basic way, and two had not included it at all. In general, the relative neglect of media issues in child protection management is quite worrying because of the strong influence the media exerts on public opinion concerning child abuse, and the consequent influence on government policies.

20) Ethnicity, culture and language. (paras 1.5 - 1.6, 5.6, 5.14.8, 6.27); Welsh language issues.

Working Together makes no mention of the Welsh language issue, surprisingly since as well as being the first language of many thousands of service users it is an official language in a substantial part of the area of England and Wales. However, issues of race, religion, language and culture are referred to in a way which generally reflects the content of the Children Act 1989, for instance section 22 (5)(c). The guidance refers to the need to seek specialist advice on issues of race and culture, and especially in situations involving children whose first language is not English.

Two of the eight handbooks made no mention of either ethnicity or language issues at all. Both issues were addressed in each of the remaining six. As regards ethnicity, very few gave the material more than the briefest coverage. Two handbooks specifically suggested seeking specialist advice on race and cultural issues when dealing with a child or family from an ethnic minority background. In only one was it noted that ethnic background details are included on the child protection register. The same handbook was also the only one to describe a duty on the conference chair to 'deal with remarks of a sexist or racist nature'.

Although six handbooks referred to language issues in the broadest sense, as noted earlier, only one handbook in Welsh was received by the team. It is important for a distinction to be made between ethnic minority language issues and Welsh language issues, as they have different legal contexts and require very different positive actions. Two of the handbooks addressed issues of Welsh language in a positive way, for example emphasising that for parents whose first language is Welsh, this should be the language of the conference, with translations provided for monolingual English speakers. These handbooks also acknowledged that 'some families may be disadvantaged by having to speak in the English language and, therefore, every effort should be made to conduct the conference in the Welsh language', and that the case conference should be 'conducted in the language of choice of the parents/child. The language of the minutes should reflect this choice'.

For three quarters of the local procedures handbooks in Wales to ignore the issue of Welsh language however, is clearly very disturbing. These findings echoed that of Colton, Drury and Williams (1994), who found that the majority of social services departments in Wales paid insufficient attention to the linguistic and cultural needs of Welsh-speaking people, and even seemed to regard the requirements in the Children Act about cultural, ethnic and linguistic needs as not applying to them.

Summary

Chapter 6 considered the role of local procedures handbooks developed by ACPCs as a means of ensuring that practice at operational level reflects official child protection policy. We began with a consideration of the provisions in *Working Together* concerning handbooks. We then described a study of local procedures handbooks which was undertaken as part of the Welsh Office review. All eight handbooks in Wales were analysed by looking at the content of twenty particular subject areas. Areas that were found to be well covered were requirements for registration, the child's involvement in child protection conferences, criteria for deregistration, what agencies should do in individual cases, and core groups. The least well covered issues were appeals and complaints procedures, written reports for conferences, media policy, criteria for joint investigation, and female genital mutilation. There were considerable variations in how ACPCs addressed criteria for exclusion from the child protection conference, and some departure from the guidance on the issue of legal proceedings not being an impediment to attendance.

Each of the subject areas was analysed by comparing the material in the handbooks with the content of *Working Together*. Comparison was based on the extent to which the material conformed with guidance and on the fullness of the coverage of the material.

7 Reforms, restructuring, reorganisation and other forms of chaos

We trained very hard, but it seemed that every time we were beginning to form into teams, we would be reorganised. I was to learn later in life that we tend to meet any new situation by reorganising and a wonderful method it can be for creating the illusion of progress, while producing confusion, inefficiency and demoralisation [Caius Petronius, AD 66]

The last ten years have seen unprecedented changes in the roles, functions and structures of the agencies who are members of Area Child Protection Committees. Mostly, these changes have been *decentralizing* in that they have involved a devolution of decision making authority to progressively more localised levels of management. There is scarcely a member agency who has not been affected, either directly or indirectly. Whilst some of the more dramatic changes in health, education and social services are common knowledge, even agencies such as probation and voluntary child care organisations have had major changes to cope with. The probation service has experienced a major shift in orientation, most recently evidenced by the Home Office's removal of the Diploma in Social Work as the required qualification for practice. Voluntary child care agencies have had to cope with the shift to the 'contract culture' and service agreements (with local government bodies which are of course themselves undergoing major transitions). For the voluntaries, this process combined with a substantial loss of revenue especially since the introduction of the National Lottery, has created considerable financial difficulties.

In Wales at the time we undertook our research for the Welsh Office, agencies were facing changes in the boundaries of police and health authorities, as well as the wholesale reorganisation of local government into unitary authorities. Managing child protection services through all of these changes presents a major challenge for ACPCs. The interagency management of child protection services, as we have seen, incorporates several sources of tension. There is the tension between those agencies for whom child protection is a major responsibility, and those for whom it is an additional consideration to their main areas of responsibility. There is the tension between those whose interest in the protection of children is largely around the investigative process and those whose interests are more likely to be concerned with prevention and treatment. There is the tension between agencies who have a high degree of centralisation in their decision making, such as social services and police, those who have considerable autonomy, such as schools and general practitioners, and those who are somewhere in the middle.

The degree of harmony and cooperation that currently appears to exist in ACPCs, as described by our respondents, is a recent phenomenon and cannot be assumed to be robust. To a great extent it has been achieved through the powers of persuasion of individuals, who have succeeded in getting others to accept concerns and priorities in child protection that they may not have otherwise had. In the words of one officer of a local education authority: 'We're all child protection agencies now.' A great deal has been achieved as a result of continuity in personal working relationships. These factors are at risk of being upset in times of reorganisation, with the consequent danger of a return to relationships characterised by distrust and suspicion.

The potential for increased risk to children in these circumstances is something of which we have found ACPC members to be acutely aware. They see risk in the disruption to the lines of communication between professionals, which has been shown to be a significant problem time and again in child death inquiries, or less dramatically in the discontinuity of worker involvement with a child and his or her family which may result in a poorer if not necessarily a fatal outcome. Colton, Roberts and Sanders (1996) in their study of Part 8 reviews were concerned at the large numbers of professionals sometimes involved with families because of the proliferation of agencies and changes of staff.

In this chapter we explore three particular sets of changes that have affected Area Child Protection Committees: education reforms, health reforms, and local government reorganisation. In each case, we begin with a description of the changes, followed by an account of perceptions of their actual or potential impact. These accounts are based on the conversations we had as part of the Welsh Office review, when we asked interviewees explicitly about their views of these changes (see Appendix A, questions 18 and 20; Appendix B question 8) or when, as often, they spoke without prompting about their concerns.

The education reforms

Whilst the Education Reform Act 1988 has not been generally described in the same expansive language as other recent pieces of social legislation such as the Children Act 1989 or the National Health Service and Community Care Act 1990, in many respects it is equally far reaching and comprehensive. The changes it heralded have had a similarly dramatic impact on the nature of the education service as those other Acts had on children's services and the health and community care services. Indeed, one writer has described it as 'seismic law-making in education' (Morris, 1990, p. 2).

In keeping with the government's philosophy the Act 'laid the basis for the privatisation of the system and for creating the conditions for a market in education' (Simon and Chitty, 1993). In addition to the introduction of the National Curriculum, with its emphasis on assessment and testing, and the consequent 'league tables' of school results, it introduced major changes in the management of schools. The most significant changes affecting the work of child protection services are probably: the decentralisation of funding and decision making from local education authorities to schools; the delegation of school management to governing boards (LMS or 'local management of schools'); the consequent diminution of the role of local education authorities which has also meant a reduction in staff within those authorities; and the introduction of grant-maintained schools, which are not funded via the local authority, but directly from government grants.

A number of writers have commented on the diminishing role of local education authorities. Fallon (1991) suggests that the only functions remaining to LEAs are responsibility for school attendance, the provision of statements for pupils with learning difficulties, auditing and inspection of schools (where further reductions in the authorities' role were planned), and planning and providing for capital spending. Higgins (1993) concludes that 'advocacy/arbitration is the residual role of the authority'. Brighouse (1991) has commented that 'in the management cycle... the LEA has much diminished power in planning, organising, providing and maintaining'. Other writers are even more pessimistic about the future of LEAs. Brynin (1993, p. 177) notes that 'the purpose of LMS is negative: the elimination of LEAs'. Hutchinson (1993) considers that the end of LEAs is inevitable, although the timescale is uncertain, and advocates for the urgent development of other structures that will ensure that schools work together rather than against each other. Maden, (1993) describes the impact of education reforms as virtual dissolution of the LEAs. Rose (1994) projected that in that year approximately 90 per cent of education funds would go directly to schools. The NSPCC inquiry into prevention has commented on LMS as making it, ' ... difficult for local education authorities to employ a coherent approach to policy and practice' (Lord Williams of Mostyn, 1996, p. 60).

The concerns that ACPC members have about the education reforms fall broadly into four categories. First is the lack of emphasis given to child protection within the education service. Second is the greater difficulty of ensuring consistency of practice and adherence to policy within the education service as a result of the relative autonomy of schools. Third is the isolation of headteachers who act as ACPC representatives from their colleagues. Finally there are the major difficulties in ensuring access of teachers to child protection training, as a result of which most teachers are thought to have very little if any of even the most basic training in recognising abuse.

Lack of emphasis on child protection in the education service

Child protection does not have the same high profile within the education service, and especially within schools, as it does for other agencies, particularly those agencies who are principally involved in the investigation of suspected abuse. This is certainly the perception held by representatives of other agencies who spoke to us:

> Schools have an agenda which puts child protection on the back burner

and:

> Child abuse is inconvenient to some schools.

were typical comments.

This is not a reflection of a lack of good will or commitment on the part of particular individuals, but as a result of the organisational constraints within which teachers, headteachers, and LEA staff operate. Because of the sheer amount of time that children spend in school, the extent to which teachers get to know children, the potential role of schools in preventing child abuse, for instance through 'keep safe' programmes, and their role in educating older children for parenthood, the potential of education services within child protection is widely understood and acknowledged. Whitfield (1987) and Maher (1987) have respectively highlighted the importance of strategies for prevention within education and the role of schools in working proactively to reduce levels of child abuse.

However, the pressures on schools produced by the introduction of local management in a context of diminishing resources, by the requirements of the national curriculum and testing, and not least by the constant attacks on the morale of the teaching profession, mean that it is increasingly hard for sufficient time and attention to be given to child protection issues. In fact, the 'pastoral' work of schools in general is under pressure, with less staff time available for anything other than 'core' functions. The huge increase in the incidence of children's exclusion from school in the last few years is clear evidence of a change in climate (Blyth and Milner, 1993; Brodie, 1995; Parsons, 1996).

Difficulties created by the relative autonomy of schools

This factor applies both to state schools where local management has been introduced and those which have opted for grant-maintained status. It is clear that the ability of local education authorities to instruct schools, for instance in what policies and procedures to follow, has been significantly affected. The observations to which we referred earlier (Fallon, 1991; Higgins, 1993; Brighouse, 1991; Hutchinson, 1993; Brynin, 1993; Maden, 1993) are echoed by the comments of ACPC members who spoke of the:

> ... withering of role and responsibilities of the education authority ... [there is] no way they can influence policies for schools.

Another respondent described the change as being one in which the local education authority has gone from being a dictatorial father figure to being a benevolent grandfather figure! The ability of local education authorities to sustain positive good working relationships with their 'family of schools' after LMS is likely to be based at least for a time on the good relationships that had been developed before the introduction of LMS and grant-maintained status. It cannot be assumed that such good relationships will be maintained in the decentralised education system of the future, especially if there is high staff turnover in schools as well as staff reductions in the local education authorities.

A further difficulty is the role of the governing bodies in child protection matters. One ACPC member we interviewed commented that:

> ...because they have so many powers, they don't accept that there are some powers that they don't have.

We noted earlier that handbooks for school governors generally fail to mention child protection or work with social services. In one case where a child was abused by a teacher it was thought that the governors had seen the issue as a disciplinary, not a child protection, matter. In fact, this general issue of professional abuse was one that presented considerable challenges for ACPCs, not least because of the difficulties presented for the education services. The risk of allegations against teachers can make the ordinary day-to-day job of teaching much more difficult, in part because of the measures teachers have to adopt in order to avoid leaving themselves open to allegations. This has included rules such as no physical contact with pupils (including attempts to comfort a distressed pupil), and leaving the door open when interviewing a pupil individually.

Isolation of headteachers acting as ACPC representatives

Not all Area Child Protection Committees have a headteacher representative, but most do. In some cases, there are two, one representing primary schools and the other representing secondary schools. Headteacher representatives, especially in primary school where they will almost invariably be the 'designated teacher' for their school, are likely to be relatively familiar with child protection procedures, and indeed are likely to be holders of the local child protection procedures handbook. However, a difficulty for headteacher representatives which we have already noted is how they are effectively to represent the views of their colleagues in other schools. Designated teachers within a given area do not meet to consider child protection issues, and headteachers collectively rarely have time to discuss child protection issues. There are of course local meetings where headteachers in a region come together to discuss common concerns, but the agenda is usually driven by curriculum and finance matters.

The net effect of this isolation is that headteacher representatives tend to represent their own individual points of view on issues that arise, and do not have a mandate from colleagues on such issues. They may sit on an ACPC in effect as representatives from their particular school, perhaps being knowledgeable about the needs of their particular discipline and their particular occupation when it comes to discussing child protection issues, but not really representing the views of schools within their areas. This tendency appears likely to have increased as a result of the decreasing role of the local education authority as focus for common planning and policy making, and the increase in competition between schools in an area.

We have seen that interagency training is one of the principal means whereby child protection policy is passed on to practitioners, and that it is also a means whereby working relationships between agencies are improved. Training together provides opportunities for people from different agencies to learn to appreciate the value base of others and perhaps in the process to modify their own. In short, it is hard to overstate the importance of interagency training in creating and maintaining an effective child protection service that is sensitive to the needs and feelings of children and families.

However, there are real problems in enabling teachers to share in interagency training, which have been exacerbated by the education reforms. A number of ACPC members were concerned about this:

> Schools will be obliged to pay for inservice training; will this be a priority?

> Access of teaching staff to training; sufficient numbers of teachers not being able to attend.

> They don't get as much training as everyone else.

The problem is not with the cost of the training per se; very often it is provided free of charge to agencies through interagency training organised by social services and funded by the government's child protection Training Support Programme. However, teachers are still in many cases not able to attend, simply because of the high cost of supply teaching which since the reforms falls on schools rather than being borne centrally. The devolution of management of school budgets to the school governors, has meant that governors in each school have the responsibility for balancing the needs of teachers for training of various kinds and the costs of providing this, with other staffing and equipment costs as well as all the other costs of running a school. In a period of severe reductions in public expenditure, and in particular severe underfunding of the education system, this means that governors often have a very difficult task in determining relative priorities.

In general, in-service training for teachers is provided through 'INSET' days which are set aside each term. However, such is the pressure for training on curricular issues that there is normally very little chance of incorporating child protection into these days.

The reform of the health service

In the introduction to the White Paper *Working for Patients* (Secretaries of State, 1989) Margaret Thatcher observed, 'Taken together, the proposals represent the most far reaching reform of the National Health Service in its forty year history'. These proposals were subsequently enacted in the National Health Service and Community

Care Act 1990 and implemented from 1 April 1991. The key changes introduced were:

1) The decentralisation of decision making (from regions to districts, from districts to hospitals)
2) A new self governing status for hospitals - NHS hospital trusts (which was extended to include trust status for community health services)
3) Money for patient treatment to cross administrative boundaries
4) One hundred new consultant posts over three years
5) The establishment of GP fund-holding practices
6) NHS management bodies to be streamlined - on business lines
7) Greater emphasis on audit of service quality and value for money

Some of the most important changes were those to do with the funding of patient services. As one commentator put it, 'an internal market has been created within the NHS in which the responsibility for purchasing, or commissioning services has been separated from the responsibility for providing them' (Robinson, 1994, p. 2). The principal role of the health authority has become that of procurement; they may purchase the necessary services from a range of service providers, one being NHS hospital trusts. The required services are obtained through the use of contracts and service specifications.

The overall impact of the NHS reforms has yet to be evaluated. Despite the emphasis within the reforms on quality audit, the government has been very resistant to the notion of evaluating the impact of the reforms (see Robinson, 1994). It is possible that some positive changes have come out of the reforms, which were ostensibly designed to increase patient choice and the responsiveness of services. However, a number of writers undertaking evaluative studies have found little change for the better. A study of choice of hospital (Mahon, Wilkin and Whitehouse, 1994) found little evidence of change pre- and post- reform. Another study exploring services for elderly persons in South Wales (Jones, Lester and West, 1994) looked at accessibility, choice, communication and quality and again found little change.

On the other hand, both the development of the divisions between 'purchasing' health authorities and 'providing' health trusts, and the growth of 'fundholding' general practitioner practices, have had or will have a major impact on the work of Area Child Protection Committees. The concerns that ACPC members have about the health reforms also fall broadly into four categories. Firstly, there is concern about the proliferation of agencies to be dealt with. This creates confusion as to where the responsibility for certain matters is located. It also creates communication difficulties because there are more links that need to be made. Secondly, ACPC members are specifically concerned about the role of general practitioners in child protection. General practitioners are very significant professionals in the lives of children and families where abuse has taken place, and yet for a number of reasons they are very much on the periphery of child protection. The reforms do nothing to address this and, for instance with the introduction of fundholding, may make it worse. Thirdly, there are concerns about the representation of health agencies on Area Child Protection Committees. Finally, concerns were expressed about the ability of service specifications and contracts to take account of child protection issues.

Proliferation of agencies

Because of the diversity of roles within health which are relevant to child protection (for instance nursing services, paediatrics, child psychiatry, general practitioners) the number of personnel representing health agencies on ACPCs has always been high. With the advent of the health reforms, however, health authorities have had to break themselves up into separate units for the purchase and provision of different services. The effect of this is described by one ACPC member:

> With the separation of roles, instead of one health authority you may have five trusts in the area and twenty to thirty fundholding practices, all of which develop a certain independence of function.

Table 4.3 in chapter 4 shows the large number of health personnel serving on Area Child Protection Committees (60 out of a total of 171, or 35 per cent). Similarly, table 5.1 in chapter 5 shows the highest average number of representatives on district child protection committees to be from health personnel (health - 6.5, social services, 4.9, education 2.5, and the police, 1.7).

With health service agencies as with grant-maintained schools, ACPCs have not attempted to ensure individual representation of every separate unit, which even if it could be done would probably make the ACPC unmanageable. However, many ACPC members from both within and outside of health agencies experienced considerable confusion over the reorganisation and its impact, for example:

> Confusion - when we talk about health, whether we're talking about commissioners or ... providers.

One of the difficulties created by the proliferation of more autonomous health units has been the difficulty of locating responsibility, especially for finances, for example:

> Trusts - completely confused as to what part of the authority has what responsibilities.

And once responsibility is located, securing agreement can also be a challenge:

> Funding, or major policy issues, you have to get the agreement of so many different people.

One ACPC member, a police representative, described taking several months to locate where in the health service authority could be found to take a decision to fund paediatricians to attend training provided by the police ... and several more months to get an actual decision. For senior managers who may be used to fairly 'crisp' decision making, that kind of experience can be extremely frustrating.

These difficulties with representation and knowing where to get decisions would appear to be part of a more general difficulty in communication. As one ACPC member put it:

> With previous structures communication was very much easier.

In terms of the objective of delivering an effective health service for children including an efficient child protection service, several representatives who contributed to the Welsh Office review suggested that the unification of children's health service across hospital and community boundaries would facilitate smoother communications.

Role of general practitioners in child protection

One of the ubiquitous difficulties facing Area Child Protection Committees is how to address the vexed question of increasing the involvement of general practitioners in the child protection process. This applies both in terms of managing the child protection services through ACPC involvement and involvement in the process of protecting individual children (e.g. attendance at case conferences). It is difficult to assess the impact of health reforms on general practitioner involvement because of the belief that GPs have always been somewhat autonomous, and therefore problems with their involvement have preceded the health reforms. Nevertheless, it seems clear that the reforms have not helped, and may have made an already difficult situation worse.

The main problem is that GPs are perceived by members of Area Child Protection Committees to lack accountability within child protection. It was striking how often GPs are described in terms that seemed to imply complete autonomy. One ACPC member commented that ACPCs had:

> ... no control of our GPs.

and another suggested that:

> Where they don't follow ACPC policy, the ability to ensure they do in future is extremely questionable.

Most respondents saw that their own accountability lay not directly to the ACPC but through their employing agencies which in turn constituted the ACPC. The lack of accountability of GPs is seen as due primarily to the fact that they do not have the same relationship with an employing agency.

This autonomy of GPs contributes to the well-known difficulties in relation to their attendance at child protection conferences, to the failure of some GPs to report serious sexual abuse cases, and to difficulties in getting GP representation on ACPCs. The problems of GP attendance at case conferences have been described by Simpson et al (1994) who found that out of a sample of 190 case conferences in Scotland GPs attended only 20. The government document, *Medical Responsibilities in Child Protection* was produced as an addendum to *Working Together* in an attempt to clarify some of the problems about medical involvement in child protection (Department of Health, British Medical Association and Conference of Medical Royal Colleges, 1994).

The same difficulties arise when GPs are represented on ACPCs as for headteachers; who do they represent? how are they mandated? Again, one answer would appear to be that they are there as representatives *from* their particular profession, but not as representatives *of* that profession. As it was put to us by a member on an ACPC which was fortunate to have a GP representative:

> We have a GP who represents himself.

ACPC representation

The difficulty in knowing who one represents within the health service is not confined to GPs. A paediatrician commented on ,

> ... confusion - who if anybody needs feedback and who is to do that.

Again the proliferation of agencies with relative independence of function is seen to complicate the process of being represented on the ACPC:

> Trusts all working independently really, makes representation difficult.

It is clear that the health reforms have contributed to representation difficulties for all health service representatives on the ACPC. As we observed in the Welsh Office review, a policy that all members of Area Child Protection Committees should have clear briefs and 'job descriptions' would go some way to provide greater clarity about mandates for representation and feedback arrangements.

Service specifications and contracts

Within the reformed health agencies, services are largely provided on the basis of service specifications and contracts. Accountabilities for child protection within the health agencies appear to be based less on fulfilling statutory obligations (with some exceptions) than on meeting contractual specifications about the services to be provided. In order for child protection to be prioritised within this new contract culture, its requirements would need to be incorporated into these contracts. There are indications that child protection has not been given sufficient priority, as reported by some members of ACPCs. For example:

> I'm not aware that the service specifications ... clearly define what the child protection specifications are.

102

or

Contracts haven't covered the amount of work that paediatricians have to do in child protection.

This has also been a contributory factor in the problems over attendance by GPs at case conferences which we discussed in the previous section. Since these responsibilities are not normally included in GP contracts, there may be dispute about who pays. One GP observed that:

Attending case conferences does not come as part of that contract.

And another that:

Because it's not part of our terms and conditions, it makes it easier for GPs not to attend case conferences.

Similar considerations apply to GP representation on Area Child Protection Committees, where a major obstacle is sometimes the lack of a mechanism for funding GPs to act as representatives.

Local government reorganisation

From 1 April 1996, in accordance with the Local Government (Wales) Act 1994, the local government structure in Wales of 8 county councils and 37 district councils was replaced by 22 unitary authorities, collapsing the division between the two levels, and integrating all of their previous functions. The largest unitary authority now serves a population of 300,000, and the smallest about 60,000. A similar process had previously taken place in Scotland, whereas in England the pattern of change has been far more varied, with some redrawing of boundaries, some unitary authorities being formed while other areas have been left undisturbed. In Wales, Powys has retained its former county boundary with the district authorities being amalgamated. In the other seven Welsh counties, although the smaller districts have disappeared, in every case between two and four unitary authorities have been created where previously there was one county.

As one might expect, the impact of this scale of reorganisation on the delivery of child protection services is considerable, and brought about in a number of different ways, directly and indirectly. Directly, the Area Child Protection Committees themselves needed to be reconstituted along different boundaries, usually, but not always, coterminous with the newly defined local authority boundaries. How this has been achieved is described more fully later in this chapter. Less directly, the impact on ACPCs has been through the effect on its constituent agencies. Like the health and education reforms, local government reorganisation has had a substantial impact on how ACPC members who are located within local government (that is, social services and education) carry out their functions in general, and the management of their child protection responsibilities in particular. The principal effect as far as social services and education are concerned, and therefore for Area Child Protection Committees, has been to create much smaller units of organisation. In addition, the process of reorganisation has meant far-reaching changes in personnel and responsibility at the level of senior and middle management. Because education departments are set in local authorities and education have had specific reforms targeted at them in the recent past, they have experienced a double impact of reform and reorganisation, taking place over a longer period and arguably therefore being subjected to the greatest degree of upheaval even when compared with other ACPC members.

Both social services and education departments as local government services needed to consider how to ensure the continuation of child protection services after reorganisation. This responsibility of course tended to fall primarily on social services as the lead agency under *Working Together*; yet as John Rea Price (1994) has pointed out, 'under the new legislation there will be no obligation for authorities to retain social services committees'. There have been concerns expressed about the impact of reorganisation on children's services in general, and more specifically on child protection services. Lord Elis-Thomas, in the House of Lords debate on local government reform in Wales, said with reference to Area Child Protection Committees 'I am not satisfied that we have at present... the opportunity for effective strategic planning of children's services. Therefore, I am deeply concerned that we shall not have the mechanism to enable the work of the existing child protection committees to take place.' (Hansard, 28 February 1994, p. 822).

In the period leading up to the reorganisation, transitional committees were established in order to oversee the process of change. During the final year, 'shadow' authorities elected in May 1995 began the process of managing the unitary structures (starting with the development of service delivery plans) whilst the previous local governmental bodies continued for their final year. It became very clear from early in the process of transition to the unitary authorities that the Welsh Office was not intending to provide guidance on what should be the structure of child protection services after reorganisation. As Williams (1995) noted, the position taken by the Welsh Office that the authorities themselves should design and implement the services meant there would be 'no requirement for strategic planning or consistency across Wales'. Authorities would continue of course to be responsible for providing the services outlined in *Working Together* and other government guidance, and the Welsh Office did ask for Children's Services Plans to be produced before implementation. But it was left to the transitional authorities to work out for themselves how actually to provide those services, without Welsh Office guidance.

Dobson (1995) has pointed to a number of concerns about the effects of local government reorganisation, in particular the dilution of expertise as a result of departments being too small, delays in their implementation of service plans, and excessive use of senior management time to implement the changes. Some of these were highlighted in our review for the Welsh Office, which we undertook shortly after the plans for reorganisation had been announced and at a time when there was considerable anxiety and uncertainty concerning the structure of child protection services under the new authorities. Many of our respondents were concerned at the capacity of much smaller authorities to deliver reliable services, and spoke, for example, of:

> ...enormous variation in the size, population and in their resources ... not possible easily for each unitary authority to provide the same level of services.

Another commented that:

> I wouldn't like to imagine what local politics could do to child abuse investigations.

Many current ACPC members clearly considered the idea of 22 ACPCs based on the 22 unitary authorities to be quite unthinkable, and a number of different models began to emerge. One model suggested the emergence of the ACPC as a kind of overarching body which could coordinate child protection services on a scale larger than the individual unitary authority. For example:

> The relationship between ACPC and the unitary authorities could be on a purchaser-provider basis.

another ACPC member noted that it,

> ...might be necessary for 2 or 3 unitary authorities to combine together for certain services, and child protection might be one of them.

Some individuals considered that the police or health authority boundaries could become the larger geographical basis on which child protection management would be based; however *Working Together* appears to prescribe that committees must be based on social services authority boundaries.

Whilst some ACPC members were considering that a larger coordinating structure would be the only tenable solution to the difficulties associated with smallness of scale, others were clearly presuming the contrary - that unitary authorities would ultimately be the basis for the management of child protection services - and they were considering how to prepare their District Child Protection Committees for such an eventuality. For example

> Already we are trying to pass responsibility down to the DCPC.

A further possibility, that of using independent agencies such as the NSPCC, Barnardos or NCH Action for Children to provide child protection services did not appear to be widely considered although it was a possibility that could well have been part of the debate. Others suggested that 'some unitary authorities may look to voluntary organisations to supply core services, (e.g. child abuse investigation ...) in a way that has not been seen in Wales for twenty or so years' (Butler et al, 1995, p.18); and at the time of our research it was known that at least one voluntary organisation was visiting transitional committees to explore the possibility of child protection service provision.

The concerns we heard about the impact of local government reorganisation may be considered under three headings. First, members were concerned that there would be disruption to interagency working, and that children would consequently be put at risk by the very process of reorganising. Second, concerns were expressed that the considerable expertise that has built up with the development of specialist workers in specialist teams would not be sustainable and would be lost, if not immediately then over time, as experienced workers leave the field, and new workers are not able in the new structures to achieve a similar level of expertise. Finally and from an efficiency point of view, members were concerned that there would be considerable duplication of effort between the 22 authorities.

Disruption to the current interagency working causing children to be put at risk by the process of reorganising

It was noted by some respondents that the very process of reorganisation itself could increase the risk to vulnerable children in need of protection. In general we found a positive attitude within Area Child Protection Committees about the progress that had been made in recent years to improve interagency working. Many of the respondents noted with pride the breakdowns of barriers of distrust that had been accompanied by the development of ACPCs in the period since the implementation of the Children Act 1989. Nevertheless there was concern that the good relationships that had been built up might be threatened by the process of change:

> Anything that disrupts that relationship within working at an individual level is a pity.

and

> Systems of communication will definitely come under pressure.

One ACPC member expressed great anxiety for the welfare of children in the transitional period and noted:

> Quite a few of the major child deaths have occurred at times of tremendous change.

Reder, Duncan and Gray (1993) argue for the necessity of a secure work setting in child protection, and note that several child death inquiries involved authorities in the process of reorganisation, for example Shirley Woodcock (London Borough of Hammersmith and Fulham, 1984), Susan Aukland (Department of Health and Social Security, 1975) and Lester Chapman (County Councils and Area Health Authorities of

Berkshire and Hampshire, 1979). It could be argued that what is most important is the degree of disruption to the contact between individual workers and families with whom they are working; perhaps even during a process of major organisational change it is possible for these client-worker relationships to be protected. However, the interagency collaboration at caseworker level which has been found to be so critical in many cases may be greatly enhanced or impeded by the quality of relationships between managers, and it is these which are most likely to be disrupted by organisational change.

The loss of specialist practice expertise

There has been a trend in child protection work over the last 20 years for work in all agencies to become increasingly specialised, being undertaken by workers who have developed substantial knowledge, skills and experience in the work. This is true not only for social workers but also for other professions such as police and health visiting. Within social work however, we found a concern that specialist expertise would be lost and that workers would again become responsible for a wide cross section of child care responsibilities. This situation could mean that some workers would be unable to use the skills and experience they had painstakingly acquired and that others might become involved in situations which required skills and experience which they did not possess. At least one respondent saw a :

> ... danger we could go back to being generic child care social workers.

This fear concerning the loss of specialist expertise was echoed in concerns about the management of child protection services as well. Would ACPCs based on unitary authority boundaries have sufficient child protection expertise available to them? For example one interviewee was worried that their new committee :

> ... wouldn't have the people with the specialist knowledge and experience necessary to work effectively as an ACPC.

and another envisaged a:

> ... sparse region with sparse professionals - they just couldn't cope - it just wouldn't be uniform.

In such a situation training is likely to have a vital role to play; but of course the same processes occur in training departments. As a result of the Training Support Programme following the Cleveland Inquiry (Butler-Sloss, 1988) training departments were able to become much more specialised, with staff working exclusively in child and family work or even in child protection. Smaller unitary authorities are having to return to a less specialised structure, unless they enter into consortium arrangements which few members of the new authorities seem willing to contemplate.

If ACPCs based on unitary authority boundaries were to operate within the existing *Working Together* guidance, they would need to have the same representation as they currently have. This may create difficulties for other agencies with wider boundaries such as the police or a health authority, in that the same staff might have to serve on a number of ACPCs rather than one. From the perspective of these agencies this would amount to a 'duplication of all the agencies in all the areas', which was clearly regarded as untenable (see the Audit Commission observations about unacceptably high levels of fragmentation and duplication of children's services; Audit Commission, 1994). One police representative clearly considered that from his perspective there already was too much duplication.

Another consequence of having more committees covering smaller areas could be that the representatives on those committees would be less senior. This could reduce the ability of the ACPC to command the kind of authority it currently has. It would contradict the expectation in *Working Together* that 'appointees should have sufficient authority to allow them to speak on their agencies' behalf and to make decisions to an agreed level without referral to the appointees' agencies' (para. 2.8). In effect there may have to be a 'trade-off' between seniority of representation and the greater amount of time a more junior manager may be able to devote to the responsibilities of membership.

The potential benefits

At the time of our research it was difficult for many of those to whom we spoke to be positive about local government reorganisation; and yet there are potential benefits that may offset some of the drawbacks. One benefit, as described recently (November 1996) by an assistant director of one of the newly formed unitary authorities, was the opportunity created for managers to put right certain anomalies that have arisen in the child protection structures and which were not likely to be addressed by staff who were enmeshed in the existing system. The reorganisation of child protection systems created an opportunity to 'rationalise' the system, learning from past experience and attempting to create managerial structures that will be more effective.

A second potential benefit relates to the tendency in recent years for child protection services to develop as a separate entity from other child welfare services. The desirability of this has been questioned, for example by Jones and Bilton (1994) and Colton, Williams, and Drury (1993). The necessities of operating on a smaller scale may perhaps help to encourage a more integrated approach to services for children and families. Children's Services Plans required by the Department of Health and the Welsh Office could play a useful role in this integration. The smaller scale may in this way help to bring about what has been called a 'refocusing' of children's services (ADSS/NCH Action for Children, 1996; NSPCC, 1996) and a consideration of whether *needs* should be at the centre of child protection rather than *risk*.

Finally, with the responsibility for child protection being devolved to more localised communities, it may become possible for communities to become more aware of child protection, and to begin to understand the complexities of the issues involved, rather than accepting overly simplistic prescriptions of the media. Indeed, it may be possible to establish better working relationships with local media, something which was conspicuously absent in the findings of the Welsh Office review. We might even see the beginnings of child protection becoming an activity that is 'owned' by local communities to a greater degree than at present.

That was then, this is now

In March 1996, a Welsh Office report (Social Services Inspectorate (Wales), 1996) described the provisions that had been made in Wales for the continuation of Area Child Protection Committees following local government reorganisation. In the 22 Welsh Authorities there were three types of ACPC organisation, individual ACPCs, individual ACPCs with a degree of coordination, and joint arrangements. All the single authority ACPCs, of which there are six, intend the arrangements to be permanent. Six authorities in North Wales, whilst operating autonomously, have set up a joint body, (the North Wales Regional Child Protection Forum), which acting in an advisory capacity provides an overview of good practice and disseminates information. Three authorities in West Wales have joint arrangements under what used to be a single ACPC area. Two that used to be South Glamorgan, and five that used to be in the former Gwent area have combined to form two consortium ACPCs for an initial twelve-month period. Single sets of procedures will operate in both unitary authority ACPCs and combination authority ACPCs. The report indicates that most authorities were able to settle financial arrangements, and will be able to provide management information to ACPCs. The SSI planned to review the operation after six months.

Since that report was published, the Gwent consortium ACPC has decided to disband into four new ACPCs from October 1997, fuelling concerns, particularly amongst the police and health authorities about the prospect of having to service four ACPCs instead of one and having to work to four different sets of local procedures. These developments appear to confirm some of the concerns that were anticipated. The lack of government guidance on how to develop child protection systems in the context of a decentralised local government structure, appears to have had at least two undesirable effects, a transition to smaller, and arguably less effective, ACPCs and an inconsistency (although some might more positively reframe this as diversity) of approach across Wales.

Summary

Chapter 7 has described the impact of major changes on the operation of Area Child Protection Committees, using observations from the experiences of those who sit on the committees. Although other agencies have experienced changes, three particular sets of reforms provide the focus: education reforms, health reforms and local government reorganisation. For each of these, the basic nature of the reforms was described, followed by an account of some of the concerns that ACPC members have had.

All of the changes have been of the same type, that is decentralisation of decision making, and this has created difficulties for child protection which relies as it does on effective communication networks both for the practice of protecting individual children from abuse and for the managing of services designed to protect children. Despite the anxieties and fears before the changes, and the many real difficulties experienced afterwards, the changes have not been without some potential benefits, for example, the opportunity to rationalise the service by eliminating previous anomalies, an opportunity to assist the transition to a needs-led (as opposed to risk-led) service that is more in line with the 'refocusing' objectives being set out by government, and a possibility that local communities could develop an active sense of commitment and responsibility for the recognition and prevention of child abuse.

8 Part 8 case reviews

The death of a child through abuse or neglect is an event that touches all those concerned, and that may have effects which reverberate for a long time afterwards. For the parents the sense of loss is not necessarily less because they are responsible for the child's death. For the professionals who were in direct contact with the child, their sense of loss and sadness may be mixed with extreme anxiety and stress in relation to their own careers, with the anticipation of censure both from the media and from their employing agencies. In one local authority, even before the preliminary facts were in, the Chair of the social services committee on learning through the media of the death of a child through abuse where the social services department had been involved with the family reacted angrily and perhaps injudiciously with the comment 'Heads will roll'. For staff of all agencies there may be concern over whether the agency will be considered to be at fault, and again the anticipation of strong adverse reaction from the media.   Death is by no means the only risk in child protection; there are the risks of severe post abuse consequences for the child, the risks to children and families associated with child protection intervention, the risks to individuals other than the child. Nevertheless the particular risk of fatality has come to dominate the child protection system to the extent that it is often not balanced against other risks. Instead the system has been driven towards zero tolerance for the risk of fatality. Pritchard (1993) for example states, 'the most crucial issue for child protection services is how successful or otherwise they are in their ability to prevent the deaths of children'.   In that sense the system could be described as 'death avoidant'. In the terminology of risk theory, child abuse fatality is a high consequence, low frequency risk which in the construction of child protection systems has not been balanced against high frequency, 'low' consequence risks. We have discussed elsewhere the impact of perception of risk on child protection systems (Sanders et al, 1996c; Jackson et al, 1995). The role of risk in the social construction of child abuse has been considered by Parton and colleagues (Parton, 1985; Parton et al, 1997).   By arguing against a positivist or medico-social model of abuse they have emphasised the importance of definitions and thresholds, reflecting some of the work of the Dartington team in their overview of the Department of Health commissioned reports (Department of Health, 1995).   Parton (1996) in a critique of that work notes that it fails to fully take on board the signficance of risk, which in the policy context of contemporary child protection has

111

taken on a heightened signficance because of the tension between the need for greater targeting arising from diminishing resources.

An approach based on 'safety at any cost' has had the effect of 'net widening'; of bringing more children into the child protection system in order to be more confident of not letting any through the net. Nevertheless, there is still on average one 'Part 8' review received at the Department of Health every week (James, 1994), and one is led to the unwelcome conclusion that perhaps we are very close to the lower limit of reduction in child abuse fatalities that can be achieved through refining our systems of interagency protection. As we suggest elsewhere in this book, we may have to look to other strategies to achieve further progress.

Despite these qualifications, and despite the limitations of the review process which we discuss later in this chapter, much can still be learned from the cases that 'go wrong'. Over the last twenty five years there have been over 40 major inquiries into child abuse. The lessons from these have been summarised in several government publications (Department of Health and Social Security, 1982; Department of Health, 1991b), and a very useful review by Reder, Duncan and Gray (1995). As has often been observed, a common theme running through these reports is the lack of effective interagency coordination.

Since the introduction of first 'Working Together' (Department of Health and Social Security/Welsh Office, 1988) after the Cleveland Inquiry (Butler-Sloss, 1988), Area Child Protection Committees have been required to undertake reviews of child abuse fatalities. The current guidance is contained in Part 8 of *Working Together*. Paragraph 8.1 of that document reads:

> Whenever a case involves an incident leading to the death of a child where child abuse is confirmed or suspected, or a child protection issue likely to be of major public concern arises, there should be an individual review by each agency and a composite review by the ACPC.

The objectives of these reviews are two fold: that all lessons from such cases should be learnt and incorporated into policy and procedures, and ultimately into practice, and that public concern should be allayed by the fact that a review is being undertaken. James (1994) suggests that an important purpose of Part 8 Reviews is to serve '... the needs of central government in reviewing national policies and amending Ministerial guidance' (para 2.3).

Working Together provides seven general principles to be observed in undertaking Part 8 Reviews: urgency, impartiality, thoroughness, openness, confidentiality, co-operation and resolution (para 8.4). The review process begins with the local authority informing the Department of Health, or in Wales the Welsh Office, as soon as they learn of a case which may require a review. Any agencies who learn of such a case should ensure that case files and notes relating to the child are secured and that the keeper of the child protection register and the chair of the Area Child Protection Committee are informed; it is then the responsibility of the latter to inform other agencies. Each agency should carry out an urgent review in order to establish:

a) Whether the agency child protection procedures have been followed;
b) Whether the case suggests that there is an urgent need to review those procedures;
c) Whether any other action is needed within the agency.

The agency review should establish a chronological history of agency involvement, assess whether the action taken was in line with agency policy and procedures, consider the services which were provided, and make recommendations. Staff involved in the case should be informed of the review process. The review should be separate from any possible disciplinary proceedings which may arise. Each agency should have a designated individual who has the responsibility to undertake the review, and agencies should have a clear policy on dealings with the media.

Agencies should complete their review within one month of the event, and pass it to the appropriate authority who in turn should forward it to the ACPC within seven working days. This process should not be delayed because of possible police inquiries. Within three weeks, the ACPC should produce an overview report which will set out the full facts of the case and make any proposals for change which arise from the review, including a timescale for those changes. This report should be forwarded to the Department of Health, or in Wales the Welsh Office, via the Social Services Inspectorate. This whole process should be completed within two months of the event and the ACPC should monitor the implementation of agreed changes, which should be published.

There have been several studies undertaken of Part 8 Reviews. Geoffrey James presented a 'Study of Working Together Part 8 Reports' to the National Conference of Area Child Protection Committees in 1994. Dr. Adrian Falkov (1995) produced a study for the Department of Health which explored the connection between fatal child abuse and parental psychiatric disorders. Colton, Roberts and Sanders (1996) undertook a study of all Part 8 reports presented to the Welsh Office since the implementation of the Children Act 1989. These reports are briefly summarised here.

James (1994) studied thirty case reviews under Part 8 which were completed during the period October 1991 to December 1993. The sample was selected across English Social Services Inspectorate (SSI) regions and across age bands (according to the age of the child at the time of the death or serious incident).

Table 8.1
Regions and ages (James, 1994)

	North of England	Central	South of England	London	Totals
less than 6 months	-	3	1	3	7
6 - 11 months	1	-	1	1	3
1 - 4 years	4	2	4	3	13
5 - 12 years	1	1	2(5)	1(2)	5(9)
over 12 years	2	-	-	-	2
Totals	8	6	8(11)	8(9)	30(34)

(Figures indicate the number of cases; figures in brackets indicate the number of children where this is different).

Of the 30 cases 26 were previously known to the social services department; 17 cases involved children known to be at risk; and 12 had been the focus of a child protection conference, which in 10 cases had resulted in the child's name being added to the child protection register.

The reports varied from 2000 to 40,000 words with between 4 and 99 individual recommendations. Two of the reports were considered insufficiently brief, lacking important details. Where there were a large number of recommendations, the more significant ones tended to be overshadowed by the minor ones.

The structure for reviews suggested by James is included in Appendix G. An important overview finding was that most reports concluded that existing local interagency procedures were satisfactory; it was non-compliance with the procedures which was criticised in the reports. In more detail, James considered the following consequences arising from his study. He noted that it is easier to identify the risks to children in such families than it is to ensure their safety. This is partly attributable to the fact that repeated episodes of harm, instead of increasing the concern, appear to induce professionals to believe that more serious harm is unlikely to occur. This may be compared with 'the rule of optimism' first described by Dingwall, Eekelaar and Murray (1983). James found reports noting that families living in the most disadvantaged areas may appear to be indistinguishable from neighbouring families, or even less likely to harm their children. This may be one of the difficulties confounding workers' efforts to predict which parents will abuse (and fatally so), and which will not. Finally, he noted that the increased risk when long term key workers leave, through moving away or through some reorganisation of responsibilities, may be underestimated. In addition to these consequences he identified a number of issues arising from the study, and suggested changes to the referral and investigation processes.

Parents with a mental disorder frequently appear in the reports of child abuse fatalities, and Dr. Adrian Falkov (1995) undertook to explore this in depth. He looked at 105 Part 8 Reviews received at the Department of Health during 1993 and 1994 (although five were excluded from the sample because they did not meet the criteria). Of the 100 cases, 32 contained clear evidence of formal psychiatric disorder. The remainder were either insufficiently documented or indicated no details of psychiatric disorder. In 25 cases, the perpetrator was the parent affected by mental illness, in 10 cases it was the partner (the extra cases suggesting in some instances both the perpetrator and the partner were affected by psychiatric difficulty).

According to Falkov

> A key finding was not the absence of agency input, (adult mental health services in particular), but rather an absence of effective intra and inter agency coordination, collaboration and communication ... In general a parental mental health perspective amongst child agencies was lacking and there was little emphasis on child protection and the nature of children's experiences prior to their premature deaths amongst adult services (p.20).

On behalf of the Welsh Office, Colton, Roberts and Sanders (1996) undertook a study of Part 8 reviews carried out in Wales since the implementation of the Children Act 1989. They found that the reports fell into the following groupings:

Table 8.2
Categories of part 8 reviews (Colton, Roberts and Sanders, 1996)

Type of Concern	Numbers
Fatal Abuse/Neglect by Parent	14 (15)
Suicide (young person)	2
Non Fatal Abuse/Neglect by Parent	3
Adult Sexual Abuser	2
Total	21 (22)

(Figures indicate the number of cases; figures in brackets indicate the number of children where this is different.)

Of the fourteen cases (including fifteen children) where there had been a death resulting from abuse by a parent, the children were of the following ages:

Table 8.3
Part 8 reviews - ages (Colton, Roberts and Sanders, 1996)

Age	Number
less than 6 months	6
6 - 11 months	3
1 - 4 years	3
5 - 12 years	3
over 12 years	-
Totals	15

It should be noted that this study selected all cases which had been subject to a Part 8 Review, unlike James' sample which was deliberately selected to have different ages represented.

In looking at the sample of 19 cases in which children were the focus, and excluding the two cases of adult abusers), the authors found material problems such as financial and housing concerns to be the most common characteristic of family background (8), followed by problems in the relationship between parents, usually accompanied by violence (7). After those the main background factors were parental mental health problems (5), parental delinquency and/or criminality (5), and behavioural difficulties of the child (5). Six of the children had been previously placed on the child protection register.

Using James' breakdown of 'chaotic' family structures, Colton et al found that there had been long term involvement of a number of welfare agencies in 8 of the cases, and police involvement because of domestic difficulties in 6 of the cases. Four of the children had learning difficulties, and a further four had additional special educational needs. The recommendations of the report are divided into two groups, those to do with the undertaking of Part 8 Reviews and those concerned with suggestions for improving practice in working with families. The main concerns were with: the generally very inconsistent approach to undertaking reviews, and the need for an independent element in the review process; the lack of assessment, the large numbers of professionals involved with families which tended to undermine continuity of involvement, and the sometimes peripheral involvement of medical practitioners especially general practitioners; the lack of clear plans to monitor the implementation of recommendations, and the lack of consideration for staff needs.

Limitations of Part 8 Reviews

Although Part 8 Reviews highlight lessons that need to be learnt in order to improve interagency practice, there are limitations to what they can achieve and constraints that prevent them from being more effective. We have highlighted a number of these including the lack of attention given to the causes of fatalities, difficulties in interagency cooperation, insufficient emphasis on monitoring, lack of comparison, and

116

insufficient consideration given to the impact on staff of the fatality and the subsequent review process.

1. Lack of attempt to understand causes

Firstly, and perhaps most importantly, Part 8 Reviews do not attempt to address the causes of abuse or of fatality. The question 'why?' appears to be secondary to the question whether or not procedures were followed. This is because of the restrictive nature of the terms of reference for a review in *Working Together* 8.5. It is not surprising therefore that there is often very little information that might be helpful to understand why a child was fatally abused; there is generally only a description of what the agencies did, and considerations of what could have been done better; in many cases irrespective of whether those actions are seen as playing a role in the fatality. It is surprising to find the extent to which important basic information about the children and their families was either completely missing, or could only be put together to form an overall picture by assembling components from the reports of the different agencies. The use of genograms and other structured assessment tools is very rare, which is surprising considering their value in understanding such families (Reder, Duncan and Gray, 1993) and the role that they can play in assessment of families in the child protection system (Department of Health, 1988).

Although not, then, appearing to address issues of causality, most reviews do attempt to grasp the nettle of how predictable the abusive incident or fatality was. In many cases reviews have concluded that despite practice which may have been good or poor, the actual incident was unavoidable or unforeseeable.

2. Lack of interagency cooperation

The usefulness of Part 8 reviews in deriving valid lessons for future practice may be severely impaired by the unwillingness of agencies to take part in the Review process. Interagency relationships in child protection are fraught with difficulty under ordinary circumstances. Hallett and Birchall (1992) provide a comprehensive account of facilitators and inhibitors to interagency coordination. Some inhibitors to good interagency coordination include, for example, incompatible values and goals, lack of clarity as to how to achieve the objectives of coordination, differences in style of operation, discrepant planning and financial cycles, differences in styles of operation and fears of loss of autonomy (Broskowski et al, 1982; Norton and Rogers, 1981). Jackson et al (1994) however, found interagency relationships on the whole very good, especially between social services agencies and police, although relationships involving education agencies appeared to be generally less strong. Sanders et al (in press) identified two factors which influenced the nature of interagency relationships between ACPC members: the degree of fragmentation or decentralisation of an agency, and the extent to which the objectives of the agency were in accord with the main policy emphasis within child protection. The second factor meant that those agencies whose objectives were more in line with the emphasis in policy on the investigation of suspected child abuse had closer relationships with each other than they did with agencies who had different child protection concerns such as prevention and treatment.

It can be seen that relationships between agencies are influenced by a wide range of factors and can vary considerably. Even when they are positive, this may be precarious. They can become much more strained at the time of a fatality when there is a high probability of unfavourable media coverage. At such times there is an even greater likelihood of a 'cover-your-back' approach, and participation in the review process may become strained, even if it is not refused outright. For example, one study of Part 8 reviews reported two cases of a mother committing suicide with a child; in one case, two children. In one of the case reviews there was a very full account of the role of the psychiatric services prior to the event. In the other, there was no input at all into the review concerning the adult psychiatric services, even though it was known that the mother had been seen by a psychiatrist.

3. Lack of detail on monitoring

It is impossible to determine from the reading of the reports whether reviews have actually improved practice, and what evidence there is of this. That in itself is not surprising. Whilst it is generally clear what specific recommendations are being made as a result of the review - and in some cases this could be more clearly set out - it is usually less clear what arrangements are being made to monitor the implementation of these recommendations. In order to complete the process of the review there would need to be internal and external monitoring systems to ensure all of the recommendations are implemented and evaluated in terms of impact and effectiveness. These should be on several different levels: agencies should have procedures for ensuring that recommendations relating to their practice and management are implemented and evaluated; ACPCs should have procedures for ensuring that the interagency recommendations are implemented and evaluated; and finally, the Social Services Inspectorate should have arrangements apart from inspection whereby they can monitor the implementation and recommendations arising from all Part 8 Reviews.

These concerns relate to our general observations on the effectiveness of ACPCs (see also Jackson et al, 1994). Monitoring, and quality control mechanisms were conspicuously absent. One of the recommendations of the report was that greater consideration should be given to quality control in the management of child protection services. It is, after all, an essential component of good practice in management.

4. Lack of comparison in Part 8 Reviews

Whilst there are considerable benefits to the undertaking of Part 8 Reviews, it is often difficult to know how extensive are the issues identified within agencies. In one Review examined by Colton et al a particular district was identified as needing significant changes to its child protection practice in order to conform with the expectations of the ACPC. The authors however could only speculate on the extent to which other districts had significantly superior practice.

This particular drawback could be remedied in one of two ways. When Part 8 Reviews are undertaken, a matched case could be identified and reviewed at the same time, providing a basis for comparison. In such circumstances important differences and similarities of practice could be observed, as well as being assessed against a standard of whether the practice was of a reasonable standard. A difficulty with the conclusions derived from Part 8 Reviews is that they rest on the assumption that the fatality was attributable to whatever bad practice has been identified; this may be true, but equally it may not. Comparisons would at least help to identify which differences in practice appear to be significant.

A second, and probably more effective, means to address the same problem would be to through a system of random audit. Under such a procedure, child protection cases within agencies are randomly selected for review. The audit is based on previously identified standards and the practice is compared with what is expected according to those standards. A useful indicator as to the type of standards required is provided by the Social Services Inspectorate in *Evaluating Performance in Child Protection* (Social Services Inspectorate/Department of Health, 1993). This document contains 21 dimensions of child protection performance, each of which contains clearly defined standards to be achieved, and within those standards criteria to be used as indicators of success in achieving them. Using such a quality control process on randomly selected cases, over time ACPCs would be able to build up a picture of the practice in their different member agencies and an area profile highlighting geographical variations. Part 8 Reviews which were conducted against this background of information could be much more illuminating, and would also be better able to inform the process of developing standards.

5. Support to staff

As yet there has been virtually no research into the impact of a child abuse fatality on the professionals involved. Frequently workers experience considerable levels of stress and anxiety associated with both the fatality and the ensuing review, and insufficient consideration in case reviews is given to how best to support such workers. By way of anecdote, one may be aware of colleagues who have been involved in such events, and almost invariably the impact has been profound and long-term. Yet despite the knowledge that the impact can be traumatic and perhaps even traumagenic, agencies appear not to have introduced measures designed to support staff after a fatality, during and beyond the review process. In one case review studied by Colton et al, for example, it was reported that :

> There is no formal arrangement or mechanism through which members of staff involved in traumatic cases can have access to a personal counsellor ... staff involved in cases where events like the death of a child occur are bound to have deep feelings of self-doubt, guilt, remorse and grief.

and from another case review in the same study:

One final concern was that staff who were interviewed clearly remained distressed by the child's death and also did not appear to understand the need for, or the purpose of, the enquiry.

Considering that child protection services are substantially dependent on the quality of staff in the field, the more general lack of consideration given to this issue in Part 8 Reviews appears to resemble indifference. Part 8 Reviews should surely consider the needs of staff for counselling and support arising from the incidents leading to the Review, and the extent to which those needs have been addressed.

Summary

Chapter 8 began with an introduction to Part 8 reviews, which are interagency reviews undertaken by an Area Child Protection Committee following the death of a child where child abuse is confirmed or suspected or when a case raises a child protection issue which may be of major public concern. We described the way in which such reviews are undertaken and the guidance on which they are based. We reported on three studies of Part 8 reviews and discussed the principal issues raised in them. We concluded by considering some of the limitations of the Part 8 review process.

9   Children's services plans

Many of our respondents were clearly unhappy with the imbalance between child protection systems and other child welfare systems. They wanted to see the formal child protection service as part of a wider network of services for children and families, but felt in many cases that this was prevented by some very powerful factors. One is clearly the stress in official guidance on the importance of systems for identification and registration of children being harmed. Another is the extent to which child protection services appear to have a privileged claim to available resources, whereas other services have to compete in a climate of budgetary restrictions and tough measures of cost-effectiveness. A third, perhaps underlying the other two, is the inescapable feeling which most of our respondents shared that the consequences of error in child protection are significantly more serious than in any other areas of work, because of the expectations of senior managers, politicians, the press and the public.

Notwithstanding these powerful forces there seems to us, and to many of our respondents, to be a case for attempting to reintegrate child protection systems with other services to children. There will continue to be children who suffer deliberate harm and who need decisive action to protect them, but to make this our only strategy for promoting children's welfare would be rather like trying to eliminate smallpox by treating the people who had contracted it. This much is probably self-evident; what may be less obvious is how agencies can move forward from the current position to a more balanced strategy at a time when resources are scarce.

One step that we think can be taken is to extend the scope of interagency collaboration into the wider area of services to promote children's welfare. *Protecting Children in Wales* argued that the joint planning and development of services, and the arrangements for agencies to work together in individual cases, which characterise certain aspects of child protection work in England and Wales could be applied more generally. Perhaps the skills and methods which have worked so well in establishing sound practices for the investigation and monitoring of cases where children are at risk of abuse could also be useful in enabling agencies to work together to provide services to children in need and their families. During the period to which our research relates, some attempts were already being made to encourage the development of joint arrangements for the planning of children's services. We will now turn to look at those attempts, at what prompted them and at how far they have addressed the needs which we have identified. Since children's services plans are a very recent development, we will try to give a relatively full account of their origins.

Origins of children's services plans: tackling the problems in residential care

Since April 1996 local authorities in England and Wales have been required to produce children's services plans, strategic plans for the development of services for children and families. These plans, which should be developed in collaboration with other agencies and with users or potential users of service, should indicate how services relate to the needs of their area. Where did this requirement come from, and what is it intended to achieve? We will argue that children's services plans have developed as a response to several different needs and objectives, but that these are not necessarily at odds with each other.

In order to understand the development of children's services plans it is necessary to take account of three strands in the Children Act 1989 and the associated regulations and guidance. First, the Act introduced new expectations in relation to planning for individual children. The Arrangements for Placement of Children (General) Regulations 1991 and the Review of Children's Cases Regulations 1991 required agencies looking after children to make and maintain individual care plans for each child which included 'the responsible authority's immediate and long-term arrangements for the child' and plans for meeting his or her education and health care needs. Although the regulations do not use the word 'plan', the associated guidance makes it clear that the intention is that there will be a written plan for each child, based on consultation and assessment (which should if appropriate be made jointly with other agencies), and that it is this plan which is reviewed at six-monthly intervals (Department of Health, 1991d).

Secondly, attention was drawn to the need for potential users of services to have a general picture of what services might be available to them. Part One of Schedule Two to the Act required local authorities to publish information on services available to children and families including family support services, day care, accommodation and after-care. In the case of both accommodation and day care this could include provision for children not defined as 'in need'. Since the duty was to publicise not only services which local authorities provided themselves, but also where appropriate those which were available from voluntary or other statutory organisations but which the local authority had the power to provide, this could encompass a wide range of services. Implicit in this duty is the obligation to take a comprehensive view of what services are available to children and families in the area of a local authority. This duty is also supported in relation to services for young children and their families by the requirement in the Act (section 19) to undertake a review of such services.

Third, the idea of a planned network of services and resources for children and their families was introduced into legislation for the first time. For instance, local authorities were expected to recruit a range of foster carers to offer a service which reflected the needs of children in their area. This represents a departure from the view of services implied in previous child care legislation, which was very much about identifying solutions to individual problems, and placements for individual children. An overall strategy was not in any way ruled out by the legislation, and of course agencies did engage in strategic planning of services to a greater or lesser extent, but there was no explicit requirement for them to do so. Now it was no longer regarded as good enough to work on individual cases in isolation from the broader picture.

In the discussion of residential care in the Guidance published by the Department of Health when the Act was implemented in 1991, the link is explicitly made between individual plans for particular children and the overall planning of services:

> Residential care remains a vital resource, but it is essential to see it as part of the overall network of services for children. (Department of Health, 1991e, p.1)

It was in relation specifically to concerns at the perceived deficiencies of residential care that the idea of systematic planning of services began to develop further. Between the passing and implementation of the Children Act these concerns came to the fore as a result of the 'pindown' scandal in Staffordshire's children's homes (Levy and Kahan, 1991) and the case of Frank Beck in Leicestershire. The Department of Health responded with a report by Sir William Utting, outgoing head of the Social Services Inspectorate, which appeared in 1991 at the same time as the Children Act Guidance and Regulations. The report, *Children in the Public Care*, drew attention to the sentence quoted above from that guidance and commented:

> Local authorities will need to draw up strategies for the provision of children's services, which would state explicitly the role of residential care within the strategy.(Department of Health, 1991a, paragraph 4.17)

Utting accordingly recommended that:

> The Secretary of State issue a direction requiring local authorities to produce and publish plans for children's services; the Department of Health to issue guidance on the content of plans and monitor their implementation.(9.1)

This was the first explicit mention of a children's services plan, and it is significant that from the outset the idea of such a plan was intimately connected with the wish to do something urgently to improve the residential care service.

In fact, what followed in 1992 was not the *direction* that Sir William Utting had asked for, but a circular from the Department of Health (LAC(92)18) which merely *recommended* that local authorities should draw up children's services plans. The circular offered some guidance on the content of plans, which at the time were clearly linked to the improvement of residential care. Some time later the intention behind the 1992 plans was described by the Department of Health in more wide ranging terms: the plans 'would help to improve services for children by creating the foundation for the planning, management and review of child care services'; they would 'encourage authorities to make their policies more explicit and to ensure that resource allocations reflected policies'; they would 'encourage collaboration between the voluntary and private sector and the authorities'; they would 'assist with more effective monitoring' and make services more adaptable to changing needs (Department of Health, 1994). However, the emphasis was still implicitly on services for children looked after away from home, and there was no mention of other statutory agencies. In addition the circular only applied to England, and at the time there was no similar request to the Welsh counties to draw up plans of their own; which is presumably an indication that production of the plans was not yet regarded as an essential component of good service provision.

The link between children's services plans and the strategy to improve residential care continued with the publication of the Warner Report *Choosing with Care* (Department of Health, 1992b), as did the link between overall service planning and individual care planning. The report emphasised the need for children's homes to have both general statements of purpose and clear admission plans for individual children, and for there to be audits of needs and resources. In Wales, the publication of the Warner Report coincided with a report from the Social Services Inspectorate (Wales), *Accommodating Children*, which pointed to the need for a greater sense of purpose and coordination in the provision of children's homes. The two reports were followed by Welsh Office Circular 34/93, which asked local authorities to begin a programme of development and improvement of residential care, culminating in 'strategic plans which establish the role of each children's home within a strategic framework'. This was not an explicit call for children's services plans, although in some quarters it was interpreted as such.

Following the Warner and Utting reports, the government set up the Support Force for Children's Residential Care led by Adrianne Jones, former director of social services in Birmingham. This was established in September 1993, with a brief to assist local authorities to plan improvements including strategic planning. Using a team of experienced consultants, it assisted a number of local authorities in England and Wales to take stock of their residential services for children and to tackle issues around quality of services, training and supervision of staff, cost effectiveness, and statements of purpose, within the context of an overall strategic plan.

Refocusing attention on children in need

Adrianne Jones, along with Keith Bilton (Jones and Bilton, 1994) drew attention to the lack of coordination between agencies providing services to children and their families, and suggested that this was to the disadvantage of those in need as well as being inefficient. The report recommended that 'service delivery should be within a coordinated and cooperative framework for meeting needs agreed jointly with the other statutory agencies (such as health, housing and education) and the voluntary sector.' This suggested a much wider framework for children's service planning than hitherto. For one thing, there was no longer a concentration on residential care as the focus of strategic planning; and for another, there was an implication that agencies other than social services could be full partners in the planning process, rather than merely being consulted.

This wider remit and emphasis on closer collaboration were also features of the recommendations of the Audit Commission when it undertook a study of the coordination of what it interestingly called 'community child health and social services for children in need'. The report (Audit Commission, 1994) drew attention to the lack of any coordinated planning of services for children in need and to the extent to which social work services in particular had, in a largely unplanned and uncosted way, become dominated by child protection. It recommended that children's services plans should be developed collaboratively by a range of agencies including voluntary bodies and local authority housing, highways and leisure departments, that 'a method should also be found to incorporate the views of service users,' and that the plan should be 'jointly published by health, social services and education' (pp 37-8).

In *Protecting Children in Wales* we repeated some of these arguments for greater coordination and noted that plans had still not been asked for from local authorities in Wales. No doubt by coincidence, the following month saw the appearance of Welsh Office Circular 11/94, which was intended 'To seek the production of comprehensive plans for children's services by local authorities in Wales by 31 March 1995 at the latest.' The circular specified that plans were to address the needs of children looked after, children with a disability, children on the child protection register, children leaving care, young offenders, families in need of support, and adoptive and alternative families. Plans were to be drawn up in collaboration with other statutory and voluntary agencies and to be linked with social care plans and children's day care reviews.

The following year Colton, Drury and Williams (1995) reported on their three year study for the government and the local authorities of services for children in need in Wales. The report pointed to a marked absence of coordinated planning of family support services and a lack of agreed definitions of priorities. In many cases social workers providing services to families had little idea what their agency's policies were and in effect set priorities themselves on an individual basis. The government responded to this research positively, largely in terms of how local authorities could better plan their services. However, the argument that services for children and families should be planned jointly was now being more forcefully put.

Also in 1995 the Department of Health published a summary of the series of child protection studies (Department of Health, 1995) which it had commissioned as a result of the Cleveland Inquiry (Butler-Sloss, 1988) and other inquiries. Several of the studies, in particular one by Jane Gibbons and colleagues into what happened to child protection referrals, appeared to support the view that there was too much emphasis on child protection investigations at the expense of providing responsive services to families where children were in need (Gibbons, Conroy and Bell, 1995). This happened on an individual basis: a family might be investigated through formal child abuse procedures and, if the conclusion was that action to protect a child was not needed, then often no further services were provided even though the family appeared to the researchers to be in need of assistance; or a family might be so upset by the investigation process that they were unwilling to accept further help (see also Cleaver and Freeman, 1995). It also happened on a wider scale in that resources, especially staff time, which were taken up by child protection work were then not available for other kinds of services. The Audit Commission proposal, that there should in effect be a strategic shift of resources from child protection investigation to family support services, was forcefully echoed in these reports.

In addition to the original objectives of improving planning for individual children and addressing the problems in residential care, there was now an expectation that children's services plans would lead to improved coordination between agencies, greater cost-effectiveness, and even a shift in the balance of service provision from child protection to support for children in need and their families. A great deal was therefore expected of the new arrangement, which was still largely untried and not yet a statutory requirement. In addition it was being introduced at a time when most of the agencies involved were continuing to have difficulties in budgeting for existing services.

There was also some ambiguity as to which were the real objectives of the planning process. Was it to coordinate what was already being provided and eliminate duplication, or to stimulate innovation? These objectives are not necessarily irreconcilable, but it may be important to know where the emphasis lies. Was it intended that the process of strategic planning would move services in a particular direction nationally, or was it more important to respond to local needs, local circumstances and the views of users? Was the principal function of the plan to put local authority services on a sound footing, especially the residential services which had given so much concern, or did collaboration really mean that the aim should be a joint strategy to which a number of agencies were committed? Linked with the previous question, should the scope of the plan be held to 'children in need' in the terms of Part Three of the Children Act, or would a wider definition be more appropriate?

Introduction of a statutory requirement

In July 1995 the government announced that there would be an order amending Schedule Two of the Children Act 1989 to require the production of children's services plans. Shortly afterwards two reports appeared which attempted to take stock of what had been achieved so far and to give advice on the direction of future planning. In England the Social Services Inspectorate Report *Children's Services Plans 1993/94* reviewed the plans produced to date on the basis of a sample of 45 plans following a national survey in July 1993 (Social Services Inspectorate, 1995). It suggested that most authorities had seen the exercise as an opportunity to take stock of their own services, rather than setting out a broad strategy for the future. They had most frequently used 'the SSD definition of children in need as a foundation for establishing their scope' (p.4) and they had in general not followed the Department of Health's advice that residential child care should be given prominence. The report comments sympathetically that concentrating on a particular service in this way 'might have been felt to distort an approach to planning which defined scope in terms of children in need' (p. 4) although it went on to advise that attention should be given to ensure that such specialised services were not overlooked. The report noted that a number of different approaches to cooperative planning were in evidence, depending in part on agencies' priorities at different times. It suggested that where agencies attempted to cooperate in mapping current needs, this was difficult because of the lack of shared definitions, databases and systems of analysis. Not all plans included clear strategies for achieving declared objectives, and only a minority proposed innovative developments; and where they did so these were 'nearly always restricted' to SSD initiatives (p. 10).

In the introduction to the report the Minister at the time, John Bowis, indicated that he wanted 'to encourage local authorities to consider widening the scope of Children's Services Plans to take account of Citizens Charter principles, the views of users and the UN Convention on the Rights of the Child so that they become comprehensive planning statements'.

A similar report from the Social Services Inspectorate (Wales), 'Preparing Children's Services Plans', gave the conclusions of an inspection of the plans produced by the eight Welsh county councils. The report stressed the importance of consultation with other agencies, with the independent sector and with children and families (although this emphasis had only recently been reflected in Welsh Office guidance). Like the English report it identified more than one approach to cooperation with other agencies, which it classified in terms of 'two broad approaches to consultation'. In one providers were involved at an early stage, needs and existing services were jointly identified, and 'in some cases aspirations for service development [were] jointly established' suggesting 'a common ownership of the plan'. In the other, plans were substantially produced by the SSD before consulting with other agencies (p. 12). It also suggested that planning was more likely to be collaborative in relation to areas of service which were themselves provided collaboratively, such as child protection, youth justice and services for children with disabilities. However, the report also pointed out that few plans made 'any reference to strategies for children with special educational needs or to joint plans for children not at school', suggesting that collaboration with the education service may have been particularly weak (p. 13). It found 'little evidence... that children and families had directly participated in the planning process' (p. 13). The report suggested that plans should 'reflect the United Nations Convention on the Rights of the Child' although this had not previously been asked of local authorities. It also suggested that plans should be based on an 'audit of need' and gave some advice on how this should be undertaken. Further advice was included in a working party report published at the same time (Association of Directors of Social Services (Wales)/Social Services Inspectorate (Wales)/Social Information Systems, 1995).

In March 1996 The Children Act 1989 (Amendment) (Childrens Services Planning) Order was finally made. It amended Schedule Two of the Children Act 1989 to require every local authority to review services for children in need and looked after. They were required to prepare and publish plans for the provision of services under Part III by 31 March 1997 and to review those plans 'from time to time'. On 1 April Welsh Office Circular 20/96 introduced the new order to the 22 new Welsh authorities which took office on the same day. The circular emphasised the importance of interagency collaboration and at the same time of making links between children's services plans and the other reviews and plans which local authorities had to undertake, such as reviews of day care provision for children under eight. It also stressed the need to involve the voluntary and private sectors, and the importance of consulting service users.

Five years on from Sir William Utting's original recommendation, statutory children's services plans had finally arrived. In addition, for the first time the same action was expected from local authorities both in England and in Wales. What were the principal aims of the statutory planning process, and what advice has been given to accompany the new order?

To accompany the new order the government published 'Children's Services Planning: Guidance', significantly a joint publication of the Department of Health and the Department for Education and Employment. The guidance is brief and fairly general. As promised, it links children's services plans to the UN Convention on the Rights of the Child and to the Citizen's Charter. It defines the scope of plans in terms of:

- Services for children with disabilities
- Services for children and young people with mental health problems
- Services for children under 8 (day care)
- Services for looked after children
- Young runaways
- Adoption
- Services for young people leaving care
- Family support to children in need and child protection
- Young carers
- Services for children and young people in conflict with the law.

It is striking that child protection appears some way down the list and is coupled with family support to children in need. What seems to be a deliberate downplaying of child protection concerns in relation to the new plans is presumably intended to reinforce the point made by the Audit Commission (1994) and in *Child Protection: Messages from Research* (Department of Health, 1995) that child protection issues should not dominate the agenda and should be more closely linked with questions of support to families. However, it may also be an indication that collaborative arrangements for child protection are still expected to take place principally in the Area Child Protection Committees.

In relation to the process of producing children's services plans, the guidance emphasises the importance of consultation with service users and with local communities. It stresses that plans should reflect interagency cooperation and that this should include shared definitions of need and agreed measures of the extent of need. It also suggests that plans should incorporate arrangements for monitoring and feedback which are related to the objectives set out in the plans.

In Wales the 1996 circular was accompanied by two other documents. One was the report of the SSI (Wales) inspection of planning documents discussed above. The other was a report entitled *Defining, Managing and Monitoring Services for Children in Need in Wales*. It had been produced by a working group which had been set up following the report of Matthew Colton and colleagues, and included representatives of the ADSS, SSI(Wales), and Social Information Systems. The report proposed a framework for developing services and defining priorities for children in need. Notwithstanding the emphasis in all other recent guidance on a collaborative approach, on joint identification of needs and on joint planning by agencies, this particular report is aimed very specifically at social services departments.

A more extensive and perhaps more imaginative initiative to achieve similar objectives is the work by Michael Little of the Dartington Unit in collaboration with the Support Force for Children's Residential Care on *Matching Needs and Resources: How to Audit Provision for Children Looked After by Local Authorities*. The package provides tools which enable agency staff to undertake an in-depth analysis of how services relate to perceived need. The package is presently in draft form but has been tried by a small number of local authorities with positive results (personal communications).

Concluding comments

It will be seen that the thinking behind children's services plans has changed considerably since 1991 and 1992. The initial emphasis on residential care has given way to an increasingly global view of planning for children in need (with the recent Department of Health guidance even hinting at taking the scope of planning beyond 'children in need' to all children). At the same time the idea of a strategy to develop in a particular direction, as indicated by Utting and Warner, has given way to a stress on identifying and assessing need and planning for services to be matched to needs. However, there is now another source of pressure for a shift of strategy in a particular direction, in the demand for a change in emphasis or as the Department of Health rather charmingly calls it, a 'refocusing' of services, between support for children in need and child protection. One issue which remains to be resolved is that of how far children's services plans are about achieving certain national policy objectives at a local level on the one hand, and on the other of how far they are about ensuring that services respond to local needs and priorities as perceived by local providers and consumers.

Another theme is that of collaboration. Interagency planning has come to be emphasised more and more, together with some hints that plans should be aiming for a 'mixed economy' of provision - although this has never been given anything like the emphasis it has in community care planning. Clearly there will still be a place for local authority social services departments to have their own strategic needs-based plans for their care and accommodation services, and this is reflected in initiatives like

Defining, Managing and Monitoring Services for Children in Need in Wales and *Matching Needs and Resources*. Such planning is not only a social services issue. Children looked after by local authorities are a corporate responsibility, and they continue to need education and health care. It also needs to link intelligently with wider children's service planning. However, it is in important respects distinct from the process of producing global strategic plans for children with a wide variety of needs for assistance, most of whom remain with their own families. This planning *must* be collaborative and it must be able to be coherent and consistent with the plans produced by all individual agencies, and not just by social services.

User participation and even 'community' participation is also mentioned more in recent versions of the planning process, but without any real indication of how all these different professional, user and community voices are to be brought together and how decisions are to be reached if there is fundamental disagreement, for instance about priorities. This raises even more sharply the question of whose voice is going to be the loudest, and of what it really means to give social services the lead role while insisting on high levels of collaboration.

In some ways the most important issue in the long term, perhaps especially for the voluntary sector but also for health and education authorities, may be that of the scope of children's services planning and how closely it sticks to a Children Act definition of 'children in need'. There is probably a case for having a planning process which is focused on children in need as defined in section 17 of the Act. However, if agencies other than social services are to use the process as a basis for planning, then that definition may need to be broadened to include all children with special educational needs, for instance, or all children in hospital. Further, if the plans are to take account of the UN Convention and are fully to embrace voluntary organisations, then they have to look beyond those children who from time to time are identified as in need in the terms of the Act, and outward to all children. There is no contradiction if one accepts that the most effective strategy for providing for 'children in need' is to ensure that services are available for all children, in an environment which is conducive to their health and development.

However, in an environment in which the needs of children and families for basic services are immense, where demands for highly specialised and intensive services are also growing, and where all agencies are subject to severe spending restrictions, the pressure to be satisfied with a narrow definition of need may often be overwhelming. We think it is important to resist this. One very important way to resist is to ensure that both the voluntary sector, which sometimes takes a broader view of need than state organisations, and service users and community representatives whose concerns tend not to be defined by statutory provision, have a well-established place in the process. One way to reinforce this could be to give wide publicity to the planning process so that people do not need to wait to be consulted. Another way could be to give the primary responsibility for the planning process to chief executives rather than to continue to label it as a social services task.

However, it is enormously encouraging that the attempt is at last being made to plan strategically for children's services and to do so on the basis of a relatively broad definition of need and in a collaborative way. For too long collaborative arrangements have been dominated, as we have seen, by important but relatively narrow child protection concerns. In a way that failed to include the energies of many of the people and organisations whose contribution might have been valued. In our view the Children's Services Planning Order could, if implemented enthusiastically, represent the beginning of a real change.

Summary

Chapter 9 has explored how far children's services plans represent a widening of the scope of interagency collaboration. We have tried to show how the character of children's services plans has changed as the original motivation to improve practice in residential care widened to encompass concerns about the balance of child welfare services and the perceived neglect of children in need. Although children's services plans were in 1996 made a statutory obligation, there remain ambiguities about their purposes as well as real concerns about how effective they can be at a time of severe financial pressure. Nevertheless they show signs of representing a real attempt to extend a collaborative approach to the planning of children's services beyond the narrowly defined area of child protection.

10 Conclusions

We have covered a good deal of ground in this survey of the work of Area Child Protection Committees. We have looked at the antecedents and the purpose of the committees, and some of the problems which they are intended to solve. We have examined the form in which child protection policy reaches the committees and how it is understood by their members. We have studied the methods used by the committees and their constituent agencies to translate that policy into 'procedure' and then into child protection practice. We have considered what it means to be a member of a child protection committee and how the idea of 'representation' is worked out in practice. We have looked closely at the local procedural handbooks that have become such an important feature of the British child protection system and whose production accounts for so much of the work of the ACPCs. In all this we have made liberal use of the research we carried out for the Welsh Office in 1994. We have also reported on studies of Part 8 reviews of cases where things have gone wrong, including an analysis that one of us was recently involved in. Since one of the messages of *Protecting Children in Wales* was the need to introduce collaboration into the planning of children's services other than child protection, we have looked at the development of children's services plans up to the introduction of the Children's Services Planning Order in April 1996. Finally, we have begun to look more closely at a theme which emerged powerfully from our earlier research, that of the effects of organisational change on interagency work.

If at times we have appeared to repeat ourselves, this may be because what we found when we examined the interagency management of child protection from several different angles turned out to be very similar. As Jane Rowe said of the research into social work decisions in child care in the 1980s (Department of Health and Social Security, 1985) it is like looking out of different windows and seeing the same view. The same themes appeared again and again wherever we looked. Three of these themes seem to us to encapsulate most of the things we want to say about Area Child Protection Committees.

Main implications of our research

The first of these themes is that of the many difficulties which lie in the way of achieving real collaboration. Confusion between policy and procedures, between on the one hand a real sense of the underlying objectives of the child protection service leading to a choice of strategies to achieve those objectives, and on the other a simple following of instructions to the letter in order to avoid censure, is something which runs through the child protection system from the top to the bottom and which in our view often distorts thinking in management as well as in practice and may contribute to misunderstandings and disagreements. We have pointed elsewhere to the dangers inherent in substituting rigid procedures for professional judgement (Thomas, 1994). The many contradictory pressures on agency staff resulting from legislative and political demands combined with shortages of resources, often make it extremely hard to give interagency work the attention it really needs. The changing structure of many agencies and the effects of 'marketisation' of services do much to impede real collaborative work. Inefficiency and lack of a clear sense of purpose mean that often those charged with carrying on the work of Area Child Protection Committees may be very uncertain of what their powers are or what is expected of them.

Nevertheless - and this is the second of our themes - a tremendous amount has been achieved. The determination which many unsung professionals have shown in the attempt to make the system work is truly impressive. All over the country countless hours have been spent in forging effective interagency decision-making structures on the strength of the few clues and fewer resources provided by central government. In most places these work surprisingly well. Committees meet regularly; they address their key responsibilities as they understand them, often very thoroughly; they tackle potential sources of disagreement or conflict in practice, in this very difficult and sensitive area of work; they sometimes take stock of existing services and in many cases they actually develop new ones. They see that practice develops to meet new demands such as that of parental participation in case conferences. Above all, in every case they have worked together to develop effective procedures for an interagency response to suspicions and allegations of child abuse, which ensure that such cases receive prompt attention from colleagues who, although they may be from very different disciplines, work together and understand each other's concerns and responsibilities. The process of collaboration which has gone into developing these instruments, although at times it may have seemed tedious or over-elaborate, has in itself done much to improve the quality and effectiveness of relationships and to promote real 'working together'.

Our third principal theme, however, is that there are serious limitations on this success. These fundamentally derive from a limited view of child protection, which to some extent is held all the way through the system but which most importantly comes from the top, in the shape of central government, and from the climate of public and media opinion in which this work is done. Although the responsibilities of Area Child Protection Committees set out in *Working Together* include an overview of prevention and treatment services, the message that members of ACPCs take from *Working Together* as a whole and from government pronouncements in general is that what *counts* are the processes of referral, investigation, case-conferencing, registration and de-registration. If those processes are tightly defined and clearly understood by agency staff, then the committee, and the managers of its constituent agencies, will be seen to be doing their main job. As we have said, this has by and large been achieved, and it is not an insignificant achievement. It may be that, as Colin Pritchard argues, this approach to child protection represents a substantial British success story in that it is saving children's lives (Pritchard, 1992). However, his argument is disputed (for example, Creighton, 1993) and in any case we think that there is a lot more to be achieved in child protection than simply ensuring that serious incidents receive an effective coordinated response, important though that is.

At the start of our research we adopted a three-part model of child protection policy which we labelled prevention, investigation and treatment. Our work has convinced us of the usefulness of that schema, although we might now be inclined to re-order it as investigation, treatment and prevention. If we think of a hypothetical case of child abuse, this schema starts from the underlying assumption that the first priority is to conduct an investigation properly. However, it then leads us on to consider what services are available to children and their families, and indeed to abusers who may themselves need and even want treatment. Finally it brings us to question what is being done to reduce the likelihood of children being similarly abused in the future. In our view all these are proper concerns of a child protection system, and it is not possible to apportion relative weight to them. However, the effective collaboration which we have found in operation again and again in relation to the investigative process, has not yet extended with equal seriousness to services for treatment and prevention. Time and again members of child protection committees, practitioners with a wealth of experience or senior managers of service agencies, expressed to us their frustration at being compelled to focus so much of their energy on one narrow aspect of service provision, and at the compartmentalisation of child protection from other child welfare services. Many of them want to widen the scope of their collaborative activity, and welcome attempts to enable them to do this.

Messages from research

There are obvious parallels between our findings and the results of a much larger research project which was going on at the same time. We refer to the studies of child protection services commissioned by the Department of Health which were published in 1995 both as separate reports and in summary report form, (Department of Health, 1995). The consistent message from these studies was to question the *balance* of child protection activity in England and Wales. Too many cases were being defined as child protection cases and receiving a child protection response; this response tended to be separate from a 'child in need' response which seemed to be denied to many families for whom it might be helpful and appropriate. The child protection process alienated many families and made them less willing to seek or accept help. There was a lack of effective service to follow a finding that abuse had occurred.   And most fundamentally, that circumstances and parental behaviour not normally identified as abusive could be much more harmful to children's long-term development that many cases of overt and even severe abuse. The message from our research is that these imbalances and gaps in practice are reflected, even mediated, in the thinking which permeates the management of the child protection system.

Similar conclusions have been drawn from studies in other countries with a similar approach to child protection; for instance Thorpe (1994) in his study of 'careers' of children in the child protection system in Western Australia and in a Welsh county. Thorpe found some differences between the two countries in types of abuse which were reported, but also found that some patterns were very similar. In particular in both areas (a) half of referrals were not substantiated or could not be investigated; and (b) nearly half of referrals were from single-parent families. Thorpe concluded:

> The text from case records demonstrates what amounts to an activity that can perhaps best be described as policing and investigation. What is being policed are the routine parenting practices of a substantial number of people. No norm is set for minimum standards, rather the onus is on the investigators to demonstrate that allegations have substance. In that sense, the bulk of child protection work can be said to consist of enquiries into parenting behaviours. (p. 193)

He suggests that policies which are appropriate to a small number of very serious cases have been extended too widely, so that investigative approaches are being in effect used to modify parenting standards. He implies that these objectives would be better achieved by a combination of parenting education and support services. This is echoed by research in Canada into the effectiveness of 'parent mutual aid organisations', which suggests that they can be more effective than formal child protection work in achieving the same objectives and at somewhat lower cost (Cameron, 1990; Cameron and Vanderwoerd, 1997). At the same time the 'over-use' of procedures which were originally designed for extreme cases can often be counter-productive, an observation which is also made in relation to the investigation of complaints against foster carers (see Thomas, 1995). Parental hostility must be particularly hard to overcome if there is disagreement about the standards which are being applied.

In some ways what is being said is welcome, and overdue. However, caution may be needed. Practitioners are not necessarily going to welcome an attempt to turn back the clock, and it is important that the next stage in child welfare policy, because that is what this probably is, is not seen or presented as such an attempt. Researchers and policy-makers have an unfortunate habit of discovering what practitioners have known all along and offering it to them as a dramatic revelation. This does not go down well with the troops, especially when those troops are exhausted after a long march. What is now being said about widening the net, about designing systems in response to extreme cases and then applying them to ordinary ones, about creating a situation where families have to be defined as child protection cases in order to get access to services, has been said by many practitioners for at least ten years. Some of them have grown tired of saying it, especially when at times it seemed to be heresy. At seminars and workshops held to explain research findings to practitioners we have observed some scepticism and even hostility to the messages being delivered. Professionals do not want to be told that they are getting it all wrong yet again, especially by academics. There is also real concern that the baby may be in danger of disappearing with the bathwater (especially when some academics have rashly attempted to quantify the number of real babies who might be sacrificed to a 'refocusing' of priorities).

On the other hand we have also seen a real commitment to continue to improve services and even to consider radical solutions to some of the problems facing child welfare services. That commitment can be harnessed if practitioners and managers are treated with respect and if their own ideas and opinions are sought before solutions are offered. That much is elementary, perhaps. What then is it that needs to be done? It seems to us that the most important tasks are twofold: first, to find ways to reintegrate child protection with the promotion of the child's well-being at the level of policy-making and strategic planning. Second, to promote new ways of engaging families with child protection and child welfare services: both as participants in investigations and protection plans, and as the key players in prevention.

Putting the pieces together

We have discussed the extent to which certain aspects of child protection policy, those concerned with identification, investigation and registration of abuse, tended to dominate the forum of policy implementation at the expense of other aspects concerned with the prevention of abuse and with offering help in recovering from its effects - to dominate even though the members of the forum may regard these other aspects as being of equal importance. We have also argued that the whole of child protection policy has become detached from the greater body of child welfare policy with which it should be organically connected, and that the success of interagency collaboration in child protection arrangements demands that similar methods be extended to the planning of children's services generally. We have seen that local authorities are now being required to produce overall children's services plans on a collaborative basis, and at the time of writing we understand that the outgoing government is proposing that this should be a corporate responsibility, not simply a social services one. Perhaps it is not too much to hope that the process of producing these plans could provide the basis of an approach to child welfare services that absorbs the child protection system back into the mainstream.

The best children's services plans will be those into which local communities have an input alongside agencies. This has particular relevance to child protection. In our final report for the Welsh Office we commented:

> Thinking about child protection is continually developing. The focus on investigative procedures that permeates current systems could be seen to stem from an era when child abuse inquiries conducted by lawyers trooped across the pages of our newspapers in regular succession. The time has come for trying out and evaluating new approaches, particularly those which seek to

give everyone in a community a feeling of responsibility for protecting children, rather than a few designated professionals. (Jackson, Sanders and Thomas, 1994 p. 151)

The problem of mandate is a critical one for child protection workers, especially when the boundaries between acceptable and unacceptable child-rearing practices are so often unclear. One solution to the problem may be to engage the community more directly in the planning and management of the child protection system, and in setting its objectives. Even more, we must engage *families* in all the processes of protecting children. All the ACPCs which we studied had worked hard to engage parents in case conferences and reviews. In one area Family Group Conferences had been introduced into the child protection system, on the basis of agreement between all the agencies. When we remember that most children on registers remain at home and that even more remain in contact with their families, it is clear that the continued protection of children who have been harmed is highly dependent on family participation in child protection plans. In addition, effective prevention requires that families, including children, are brought into dialogue with agencies, both at the level of individual cases and more generally within communities, about what they need and how they can most effectively be helped.

In general, then, we support the argument that there should be a 're-focusing' of services, of priorities and of methods. That re-focusing has to take account of the gaps which we and others have identified in the way in which services are currently organised and provided. It will have to confront some fairly serious resourcing problems. It may also have to face some sharp moral and political dilemmas, including some questions about what it is that children most need to be protected from; which is not always what their families do or fail to do, and may often be what the state does or fails to do. However, the refocusing will also need to start by recognising what has been achieved in the last twenty years in terms of ensuring that, where serious concerns are expressed about a child, an effective, sensitive, planned and coordinated interagency response can usually be relied upon. That achievement is due in no small part to the work of Area Child Protection Committees.

A new model for interagency collaboration?

As we pointed out at the beginning of this book, what is most distinctive about the British child protection system is its highly structured approach to interagency collaboration. This is evident both in the emphasis on procedures and in the institution of Area Child Protection Committees, with their structure and operation so carefully prescribed by central government. If we are to widen the focus of interagency collaboration, not only to take in a broader view of what counts as child protection work but also to encompass a broad range of services to children and families, then attention will need to be paid to that structure.

It seems to us that it is implicit in the development of children's services plans that collaborative arrangements for child protection should be part of a wider network of collaboration to promote children's welfare, rather than an independent or free-standing institution. This is consistent with the NSPCC Commission of Inquiry into prevention (Lord Williams of Mostyn, 1996), which indicated 'The role and activities of child protection committees and area child protection committees (ACPCs) need to relate more closely to wider strategic planning and the delivery of children's services' (p.64). This could be taken to mean absorbing child protection committees into new bodies with a much wider focus. We think that this would be a mistake. Area child protection committees carry out work that is in important ways distinct from general planning of children's services, and which will continue to need a distinctive focus. However, we do think it would be valuable for Area Child Protection Committees to be organically linked to other groups engaged in planning childrens' services.

One way to do this would be to establish in each local area a 'children's committee' with overall responsibility for service planning and identification of need. The Area Child Protection Committee could become in effect a subcommittee of this group with its own delegated responsibilities, alongside other sub-groups dealing with particular areas where a specialised focus was needed. For instance, a group which focused on children looked after away from home would be able to address such matters as the deficiencies in health and education provision for children looked after by local authorities, or the neglect by all agencies of privately fostered children. A group with overall responsibility for children in need as defined by section 17 of the Children Act could begin to develop better coordinated and less stigmatising services for this ever-changing group. A group with a wider remit for general children's services could look at day care provision, bullying in schools even road safety (or better still, children's access to the streets). A subcommittee for children's rights could review implementation of the United Nations Convention and could monitor the extent to which children were given a voice in service provision.

In Figure 1 we illustrate such a possible model. It should be emphasised that this is not intended to be a fully worked-out model for a new structure, and we are not in any case convinced that prescription in detail is appropriate. There should be a degree of space for local variation and experiment in finding ways to meet objectives, although the overall objectives should be the same. What we are presenting here is one example of how the structures of collaboration could be adapted to meet some of the wider needs that we and others have identified.

It also seems to us that the emphasis on involving non-statutory organisations, local communities and user groups in the planning of children's services generally, has much to offer in reviving the preventative aspect of child protection work specifically. New structures for collaborative planning ought to have a much wider constituency than the traditional statutory agencies, and we have tried to reflect this in our model. In addition we would strongly recommend that children and young people should be included in the new structures at every point (including the new Area Child Protection Committee). Too much lip-service is paid to listening to children and young people, and too much is done *to* them or *for* them when it could be done *with* them or *by* them.

Of course, we are not suggesting that all this collaboration would necessarily be harmonious. The experience of Area Child Protection Committees is that the work to be done in establishing effective collaboration is difficult, time-consuming and sometimes painful. It often requires people to give way on matters which may be dear to their hearts or to their professional pride. Involving local communities and user groups in the planning of services such as child protection will never be easy, either for the professional agencies or for the groups themselves. We have seen that we cannot always assume that professionals will share the same attitudes, and disparities may be even greater when professionals and lay people meet together. For instance, professionals may wish to provide treatment services for abusers, when a local community may be more concerned to exclude them. However, these differences are likely to exist whether dialogue takes place or not. A forum for discussion may at least offer some hope of establishing common ground.

It might be thought perverse of us to suggest any kind of structural change after our observations in Chapter 7 on the sometimes chaotic impact of reforms, reorganisations and restructurings. However, the ways in which Area Child Protection Committees are currently established, the organisational levels at which they operate, and the operating briefs which they are given, have a very definite effect on the ways in which child protection services are organised and managed. If the balance of service provision is to change, then some structural change may be part of the price we have to pay. The kind of change we are proposing is intended to lead to greater integration, whereas many recent reorganisations have been experienced as disintegrative; and it does not threaten to disrupt the most important relationship, that between practitioners and service users.

The new committees would not of course be executive committees with responsibility for managing services; that would remain with individual agencies as it does at present in child protection. The role of the collaborative group is to coordinate, not to manage. One intention of the new structure, however, would be to ensure that child protection did not any longer stand apart from other child welfare services with its own unique arrangements for collaboration. Some may fear that this could mean a dilution of the attention currently given to child protection with a consequent risk to children. Our reply must be that enough has been done in recent years to ensure that protecting children from harm is uppermost in the minds of most service providers, to enable us with some confidence to broaden our gaze to other aspects of children's welfare, and to take more account of what children and families themselves say they need.

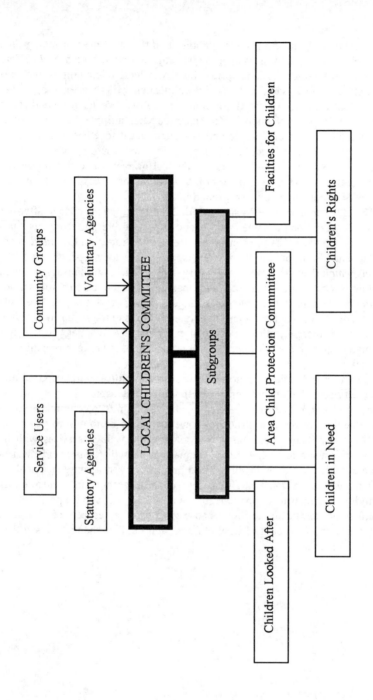

Figure 10.1: A Model for Child Welfare Services

Appendix A:
Interview schedule - ACPC
representatives

General
1. How long have you been a member of the ACPC?
2. How have you found it?
3. How were you briefed on your responsibilities as an ACPC member?

Welsh Office Policy
4. What do you consider to be the most important elements of Welsh Office Policy in child protection? (Assuming more than three elements supplied) If you had to pick three as the most important, which would you pick?
5. How is Welsh Office policy and ACPC policy communicated to the staff of your agency?

Level of Representation
6. How do you find out what people in your agency think?
7. In the last year, have you asked for an item to be put on the Agenda? What happened?
8. Before an ACPC meeting would you normally discuss the agenda with anyone within your agency? With anyone or any agencies outside your agency?
9. Can you give an example of something that you would be able to agree or act upon as an ACPC representative on your own authority?
10. Can you give an example of something on which you would need to refer back to someone else in your agency?
11. Do you feel that you are the right person to represent your agency on the ACPC?
12. Do you feel that people representing other agencies are the right persons?

ACPC Meetings: Efficiency and Effectiveness
13. Can you describe a typical ACPC meeting? (if not included above) What works well? What doesn't work so well?

14. If we look at child protection policy on a continuum from prevention through investigation and registration to treatment and after-care, where do you see ACPC concerns as falling on that continuum?

15. What percentage of ACPC meetings is given over to those different aspects?

Impact on Practice

16. How do staff of your agency attending case conferences know what is ACPC policy on registration?

17. What is your ACPC doing to promote good inter agency working at the level of practice?

Structural Changes

18. General - Recently, there have been very substantial and significant changes in the structures of agencies providing services. Has this had an effect on the ACPC?

19. Do you have District Child Protection Committees represented on the ACPC? How does that work?

20. Specific - Have specific changes affecting your agency (Education, Health, reorganisations) had an impact on the ACPC? If so, how?

Is there anything else you would like to tell us?

Appendix B:
Interview schedule - ACPC chairs

General
1. Can you describe how you see your role?

Policy
2. One of the aims of the review is to explore how policy becomes translated into practice. Using parental participation in case conferences as an example, can you describe the process through which that was developed in this ACPC area?
3. Are there any other areas of policy which have been successfully developed, and were there any difficulties you had in developing them?
4. Can you give examples of policy areas that you have wanted to develop, and not been able to?

Issues Arising From Interviews with Representatives
5. It's been suggested that some agencies may be more closely involved in the work of the committee. Would you say that was true in (county)?
   -Which agencies?
   -In what ways?
   -Why?
6. Do you find that agencies represented on your committee are represented at the right level (or have sufficient authority)?
7. In terms of your role in protecting children within (county) what are your expectations upon the Welsh Office in terms of policy and guidance?
8. In the context of Local Government Reorganisation within Wales,
   a) What are the strengths of the current system for managing child protection that you would like to see preserved?
   b) Are there opportunities you can see under LGR for improving areas of child protection management that don't work so well now?

9. ACPC Budget Information (if not already previously covered - see appendix). Does the ACPC have any influence on the budgetary priorities within its agencies? Examples?

10. District Committees

a) What are the key responsibilities of District Committees?

b) How are the DCPCs different from ACPCs?

11. Monitoring, Evaluating, Audit

a) How does the ACPC monitor the impact of its policy on practice?

b) How do the constituent ACPC members monitor the impact of ACPC policy within their agencies?

c) Is there a system of randomly selected cases for audit?

12. What do you consider has been the ACPCs most substantial contribution to the protection of children?

Is there anything else you would like to tell us?

Appendix C: Questionnaire - ACPC representatives

1. My agency (please tick the category which best describes your agency)

HEALTH	
EDUCATION	
SOCIAL SERVICES	
POLICE	

2. Please describe the following interagency working relationships (at both operational and ACPC level) along the following dimensions by circling the appropriate number:

1	2	3	4	5
Poor working relations characterised by tension, distrust, or conflict				Good working relations characterised by trust, absence of conflict, ease of communication

with 1 and 5 representing the extremes as described, and 2,3, and 4 representing intermediate points.

HEALTH - EDUCATION
Field worker relationships

1	2	3	4	5
Poor				Good

ACPC relationships

1	2	3	4	5
Poor				Good

HEALTH - SOCIAL SERVICES
Field worker relationships

1	2	3	4	5
Poor				Good

ACPC relationships

1	2	3	4	5
Poor				Good

HEALTH - POLICE
Field worker relationships

1	2	3	4	5
Poor				Good

ACPC relationships

1	2	3	4	5
Poor				Good

EDUCATION - SOCIAL SERVICES
Field worker relationships

1	2	3	4	5
Poor				Good

ACPC relationships

1	2	3	4	5
Poor				Good

EDUCATION - POLICE

Field worker relationships

1	2	3	4	5
Poor				Good

ACPC relationships

1	2	3	4	5
Poor				Good

SOCIAL SERVICES - POLICE

Field worker relationships

1	2	3	4	5
Poor				Good

ACPC relationships

1	2	3	4	5
Poor				Good

Comment: (please use the space below for any observations on the interagency working relationships arising from the questionnaire)

Appendix D:
Questionnaire - ACPC chairs

Please rate the following (by circling one of the numbers):

1. Decision making ability of representatives to ACPC

Virtually none have decision making authority	1	2	3	4	5	Virtually all have decision making authority

Comment:

2. Efficiency of ACPC meetings

Very inefficient	1	2	3	4	5	Very efficient

Comment:

3. "Ownership" of ACPC by constituent agencies

Clearly driven by one or two agencies	1	2	3	4	5	Clear sense of ownership by all agencies

Comment:

4. Degree of sharing common objectives/goals

Work of ACPC driven by negotiations over individual agency objectives	1	2	3	4	5	Work of ACPC driven by work on common objectives

Comment:

5. Monitoring impact of policy on practice
(Complete the following): "The ACPC discusses/monitors the impact of previously agreed ACPC policy..."

1	2	3	4	5
Never	Rarely	Occasionally	Frequently	Always

Comment:

6. Relationship to the Welsh Office
Contact

1	2	3	4	5
Infrequent contact				Frequent contact

Influence

1	2	3	4	5
Strong influence on local policy development				Little influence on policy development

Comment:

Please list what you consider to be the main obstacles to interagency working <u>at operational level</u>

1...
2...
3...

Please list what you consider to be the main obstacles to interagency working <u>at ACPC level</u>

1...
2...
3...

Appendix E:
District Child Protection Committee functions: An example of terms of reference

a. To receive and consider reports from initial child protection case conferences and further agency/core group/conference reports as necessary.

b. To review at regular intervals all Divisional child protection register entries and ensure there is an appropriate multi-disciplinary child protection plan agreed and implemented for each child registered.

c. To ensure unilateral action by individual agencies is not taken except in exceptional circumstances by those agencies with statutory child protection responsibilities.

d. To examine the circumstances of exceptional cases where unilateral action is taken, offer advice where appropriate and bring any significant issues arising to the attention of the ACPC.

e. To ensure that written guidance in organisation, policy and procedures is available to all relevant staff on a multi-agency basis.

f. To discuss any significant practice issues raised by individual cases and bring these to the attention of the ACPC.

g. To review the incidence of child protection referrals and the response to such referrals on an annual basis and to consider, as appropriate, the implications for policy, procedures and resources.

h. To furnish reports and statistics to the ACPC as and when requested.

i. To nominate representatives to attend the ACPC when required.

j. To identify the child protection training needs of all those involved is working with children at risk and their families, and to bring these to the attention of the ACPC as and when appropriate.

k. To act as an appeals body in cases where parents/carers and, age and understanding allowing, a child appeal against registration/de-registration by a child protection case conference.

l. To meet regularly at three monthly intervals with additional meetings as and when necessary.

Appendix F:
A specimen job description/brief

1. The title of the role represented on the Area Child Protection Committee (for example in some ACPCs there is one headteacher representative, in others there are two, one for primary schools and one for secondary schools).

2. A description of the agency/agencies whose views will be represented to ACPCs.

3. Indication of the decision making authority of the role (that is what decisions need to be referred back to the agency).

4. A description of how decisions taken at ACPCs will be fed back to the agency/agencies and how the representative will be briefed on agency view(s).

5. Expectation to attend regular meetings of the Area Child Protection Committee and special meetings as and when required.

6. Involvement in functional subcommittees where indicated by role (i.e. socials services child protection trainer would expect to be involved in a training subcommittee, perhaps chairing).

7. Involvement in District Child Protection Committees (again where indicated by the role).

8. Production of written reports from/to agency/agencies.

9. An expectation of involvement on behalf of both the agency and the ACPC in any reviews deemed necessary under Part 8 of *Working Together*.

Appendix G: A framework for part 8 reviews (James, 1994)

1. Introduction

2. The Inter-Agency Review Process

3. Family Composition

4. Chronology of events

5. Overview of the family

6. Commentary on events

7. Issues for individual agencies

8. Issues for ACPC procedures

9. Action already taken

10. Reasons whether or not an Independent Review is needed

11. Summary and recommendations

Bibliography

Association of Directors of Social Services (ADSS)/NCH Action for Children (1996), *Children Still in Need: Refocusing child protection in the context of children in need*, NCH Action for Children: London.

Association of Directors of Social Services (Wales)/Social Services Inspectorate (Wales)/Social Information Systems (1995), *Defining, Managing and Monitoring Services for Children in Need in Wales*.

Audit Commission (1994), *Seen But Not Heard: Co-ordinating Community Child Health and Social Services for Children in Need*, HMSO: London.

Baher, L. (1990), *The School Governors & Parents Handbook*, Basil Blackwell: Oxford.

Birchall, E. and Hallett, C. (1995), *Working Together in Child Protection*, HMSO: London.

Blyth, E. and Milner, J. (1993), 'Exclusion from School: A First Step in Exclusion from Society?', *Children & Society*, Vol. 7, No. 3, pp. 255-68.

Briggs, F. and Hawkins, R. (1997), *Child Protection: A guide for teachers and child care professionals*, Allen & Unwin, Australia.

Brighouse, T. (1991), 'The Uncertain Future of Local Education Authorities', *Local Government Policy Making*, Vol. 18, No.1, pp. 8-13.

British Association for Social Workers (1978), *The Central Child Abuse Register*, Birmingham, BASW.

British Association for Social Workers (1985), *The Management of Child Abuse*, Birmingham, BASW.

Brodie, I. (1995), ' Exclusion from School', Highlight No. 136, National Children's Bureau: London.

Broskowski, A., O'Brien, G. and Prevost, J. (1982), 'Interorganisational strategies for survival: looking ahead to 1990', *Administration in Mental Health*, Vol. 9, No. 3, pp. 198-210.

Brown, L. and Fuller, R. (1991), 'Central Scotland's joint police and social work initiative in child abuse: an evaluation', *Children & Society*, Vol. 5, No. 3, pp. 232-40.

Brynin, M. (1993), *Pressure on Education*, Avebury: Aldershot.

Bury, M. and Elston, M. (1987), 'Professional Collaboration and the Abuse of Children', in *After Beckford: essays on themes related to child abuse*, Department of Social Policy and Social Science, Royal Holloway and Bedford New College.

Butler, I., Davies, M. and Noyes, P. (1995*), Planning for Children: The Effects of Local Government Reorganisation*, NSPCC: London.

Butler-Sloss, E. (1988), *Report of the Inquiry into Child Abuse in Cleveland 1987*, Cmnd 412, HMSO: London.

Cameron, G. (1990), 'The potential of informal social support strategies in child welfare', in Rothery, M. and Cameron, G., *Child Maltreatment: expanding our concept of helping*, Lawrence Erlbaum: New York.

Cameron, G. and Vanderwoerd, J. (1997), *Protecting Children and Supporting Families: Promising Programs and Organizational Realities*, Aldine de Gruyter: New York.

Campbell, H. and Wigglesworth, A. (1993), 'Child protection in school: a survey of the training needs of Fife schoolteachers', *Public Health*, Vol. 107, No. 6, pp. 413-19.

Carson, D. (1996), 'Risking Legal Repercussions', chapter 1 in Kemshall, H. and Pritchard, J., *Good Practice in Risk Assessment and Risk Management*, Jessica Kingsley: London.

Cleaver, H. and Freeman, P. (1995) *Parental Perspectives in Cases of Suspected Child Abuse*, London, HMSO.

Colton, M., Drury, C. and Williams, M. (1993), Final Report on Stage 1 of Research Project on Children in Need in Wales under the Children Act 1989, Department of Social Policy and Applied Social Studies, University of Wales Swansea.

Colton, M., Drury, C. and Williams, M. (1995), *Children in Need*, Avebury: Aldershot.

Colton, M., Roberts, S. and Sanders, R. (1996), *An Analysis of Area Child Protection Committee Reviews on Child Deaths and Other Cases of Public Concern in Wales: A Report for Welsh Office*, Welsh Office: Cardiff.

Colton, M. and Vanstone, M. (1996), *Betrayal of Trust: Sexual Abuse by Men who Work with Children ... in their own words*, Free Association Books: London.

Corpe, G. (1987), 'How can registration of children protect them from abuse?' *Social Work Today*, 31 August.

The County Councils and Area Health Authorities of Berkshire and Hampshire (1979), *Lester Chapman: inquiry report*, Berkshire.

Creighton, S.J. (1993), 'Children's homicide: An exchange', *British Journal of Social Work*, Vol. 23, pp. 643-44.

Dartington Social Research Unit and Support Force for Children's Residential Care (1996), *Matching Needs and Resources: How to Audit Provision for Children Looked After by Local Authorities*.

Department of Health (1991a), *Children in the Public Care*, HMSO: London.

Department of Health (1991b), *Child Abuse: A Study of Inquiry Reports 1980 - 1989*, HMSO: London.

Department of Health (1991c), *Patterns and Outcomes in Child Placement*, HMSO: London.

Department of Health (1991d), *The Children Act 1989: Guidance and Regulations Volume 3: Family Placement*, HMSO: London.

Department of Health (1991e), *The Children Act 1989: Guidance and Regulations Volume 4: Residential Care*, HMSO: London.

Department of Health (1992a), *Child Protection: Guidance for Senior Nurses, Health Visitors, and Midwives*, HMSO: London.

Department of Health (1992b), *Choosing with Care: The Report of the Committee of Inquiry into the Selection, Development and Management of Staff in Children's Homes*, HMSO: London.

Department of Health (1994) *The UN Convention on the Right of the Child: the UK's First Report to the UN Committee on the Rights of the Child, HMSO*: London.

Department of Health (1995), *Child Protection: Messages from Research*, HMSO: London.

Department of Health (1996), *Children's Services Planning: Guidance*, HMSO: London.

Department of Health and Social Security (1974a), *Report of the Committee of Inquiry into the Care and Supervision Provided in Relation to Maria Colwell*, HMSO: London. Department of Health and Social Security (1974b), *Non-Accidental Injury to Children*, LASSL (74/13).

Department of Health and Social Security (1975), *Report of the committee of inquiry into the provision and co-ordination of services to the family of John George Aukland*, HMSO: London.

Department of Health and Social Security (1976), *Non-Accidental Injury to Children: The Police and Case Conferences*, LASSL (76/26).

Department of Health and Social Security (1980), *Child Abuse: Central Register Systems*, LASSL (80/4).

Department of Health and Social Security (1982), *Child Abuse: A Study of Inquiry Reports 1973 - 1981*, HMSO: London.

Department of Health and Social Security (1985), *Social Work Decisions in Child Care: Recent Research Findings and their Implications*, HMSO: London.

Department of Health and Social Security (1986), *Child Abuse: Working Together. A Draft Guide to Arrangements for Inter-Agency Co-operation for the Protection of Children*, HMSO: London.

Department of Health and Social Security (1988), *Working Together: A Guide to Inter-Agency Co-operation for the Protection of Children from Abuse*, HMSO: London.

Department of Health and Social Security/Welsh Office (1988), *Working Together: A guide to arrangements for inter-agency co-operation for the protection of children from abuse*, HMSO: London.

Department of Health/Social Services Inspectorate (1995), *The Challenge of Partnership in Child Protection: Practice Guide*, HMSO: London.

Department of Health/British Medical Association/Conference of Medical Royal Colleges (1994), *Child Protection: Medical Responsibilities*, HMSO: London.

Dingwall, R., Eekelaar, J. and Murray, T. (1983), *The Protection of Children: State Intervention and Family Life*, Blackwell: Oxford.

Dobson, R. (1995), 'Small Comfort', *Community Care*, 13-19 April, pp. 26-7.

Evans, M. and Miller, C. (1992), *Partnership in Child Protection: The Strategic Management Response*, National Institute for Social Work/Office for Public Management: London.

Fallon, M. (1991), Education, 26/4/91 cited in Simon, B. (1992) *What Future for Education*, Lawrence & Wishart: London.

Falkov, A. (1995), *Working Together 'Part 8' Reports - Fatal Child Abuse and Parental Psychiatric Disorder*, HMSO: London.

Fletcher, N. (1990), 'The Education Reform Act and Educational Politics', Chapter 4 in Morris, R. (1990) *Central and Local Control of Education After the Education Reform Act 1988*, Longman: Harlow.

Gibbons, J. (1997), 'Relating outcomes to objectives in child protection policy', Chapter 5 in Parton, N. (ed.) *Child Protection and Family Support: Tensions, contradictions and possibilities*, Routledge: London.

Gibbons, J., Conroy, S. and Bell, C. (1995), *Operating the Child Protection System*, HMSO: London.

Giller, H., Gormley, C. and Williams, P. (1992), *The Effectiveness of Child Protection Procedures: An Evaluation of Child Protection in Four A.C.P.C. Areas*, Social Information Systems: Manchester.

Hallett, C. (1993), 'Working Together in Child Protection', chapter 7 in Waterhouse, L., *Child Abuse and Child Abusers: Protection and Prevention*, Jessica Kingsley: London.

Hallett, C. (1995), *Inter-agency Coordination in Child Protection*, HMSO: London.

Hallett, C. and Birchall, E. (1992), *Coordination and Child Protection: A Review of the Literature*, HMSO: London.

H.M. Government (1988), *The Education Reform Act 1988, Chapter 19*, HMSO: London.

H.M. Government (1989), *The Children Act 1989, Chapter 41*, HMSO: London.

H.M. Government (1990), *The National Health Service and Community Care Act 1990*, HMSO: London.

H.M. Government (1994), *The Local Government (Wales) Act 1994, Chapter 19*, HMSO: London.

Higgins, K. (1993), 'The Local Education Authority: a disappearing phenomenon?', *Local Government Policy Making*, Vol. 19, No. 5, pp. 15-20.

Home Office/Department of Health (1992), *Memorandum of Good Practice on Video Recorded Interviews with Child Witnesses for Criminal Proceedings*, HMSO: London.

Home Office/Department of Health/Department of Education and Science/Welsh Office (1991), *Working Together Under the Children Act 1989: A guide to arrangements for inter-agency co-operation for the protection of children from abuse*, HMSO: London.

Hutchinson, G. (1993), 'To boldly go: Shaping the future without the LEA', *Local Government Policy Making*, Vol. 19, No. 5, pp. 9-14.

Jackson, S., Sanders, R. and Thomas, N. (1994), *Protecting Children in Wales: The Role and Effectiveness of Area Child Protection Committees*, University of Wales Swansea: Swansea.

Jackson, S., Sanders, R. and Thomas, N. (1995), 'Setting Priorities in Child Protection: Perception of Risk and Agency Strategy', presented at ESRC Conference: 'Risk in Organisational Settings' on 16/17 May 1995.

James, G. (1994), *Study of Working Together 'Part 8' Reports*, Discussion Report for ACPC National Conference, Department of Health: London.

Jones, A. and Bilton, K. (1994), *The Future Shape of Children's Services*, National Children's Bureau: London.

Jones, D., Lester, C. and West, R. (1994), 'Monitoring Changes in Health Services for Older People' in Robinson, R. and LeGrand, J. (eds.) (1994) *Evaluating the NHS Reforms*, Kings Fund Institute/Policy Journals: Newbury, Berkshire.

Leonard, M. (1989), *The School Governors Handbook*, Basil Blackwell: Oxford.

Levin, P. (1983), 'Teachers' perceptions, attitudes and reporting of child abuse/neglect', *Child Welfare*, Vol. 62., No. 1, pp. 14-19.

Levy, A. and Kahan, B. (1991), *The Pindown Experience and the Protection of Children: the Report of the Staffordshire Childcare Inquiry 1990*, Staffordshire County Council.

London Borough of Brent and Brent Health Authority (1985), *A Child in trust: the report of the panel of inquiry into the circumstances surrounding the death of Jasmine Beckford*, London.

London Borough of Hammersmith and Fulham (1984*), Report on the death of Shirley Woodcock*, London.

London Borough of Islington (1989), *Liam Johnson Review: Report of Panel of Inquiry*, London Borough of Islington.

Lyon, C. and de Cruz, P. (1993), *Child Abuse* (second edition), Family Law: Bristol.

Maden, M. (1993), 'Dissolution in All but Name', in Brynin, M. (1993) *Pressure on Education*, Avebury: Aldershot.

Maher, P.(1987), 'The school's proactive role in reducing levels of child abuse', chapter 11 in Maher, P. (ed.)(1987) *Child Abuse: The Educational Perspective*, Blackwell: Oxford.

Mahon, A., Wilkin, D. and Whitehouse, C. (1994), 'Choice of Hospital for Elective Surgery Referrals: GPs and Patients Views' in Robinson, R. and LeGrand, J. (eds.) (1994) *Evaluating the NHS Reforms*, Kings Fund Institute/Policy Journals: Newbury, Berkshire.

Mahoney, T. (1988), *Governing Schools: Power Issues and Practice*, Macmillan Education: Basingstoke.

Masson, J. (1994) 'Implementing the Children Act 1989: the changing relationship between local and central government' in Maclean, M. and Kurczewski, J. *Families, Politics and the Law: perspectives for East and West Europe*, Oxford: Clarendon Press.

Mills, C. and Vine, P. (1990), 'Critical Incident Reporting - an Approach to Reviewing the Investigation and Management of Child Abuse', *British Journal of Social Work*, Vol. 20, pp. 215-20.

158

Morris, R. (ed.) (1990), *Central and Local Control of Education After the Education Reform Act 1988*, Longman: Harlow.

National Society for the Prevention of Cruelty to Children (NSPCC) (1996), *Messages from the NSPCC - a contribution to the 'Refocusing Debate'*, NSPCC: London.

National Children's Bureau (1994), Children and Parliament, Issue Number 206, 9 August 1994.

Norton, A. and Rogers, S. (1981), 'The health service and local government services', in McLachlan, G. (ed.) *Matters of Moment*, Oxford University Press: London.

Parsons, C. (1995), 'Permanent Exclusions from Schools in England in the 1990s: Trends, Causes and Responses', *Children & Society*, Vol. 10, pp.177-86.

Parton, N. (1985), *The Politics of Child Abuse*, Macmillan: London.

Parton, N. (1991), *Governing the Family: Child Care, Child Protection and the State*, Macmillan: London.

Parton, N. (1996), Child protection, family support and social work: a critical appraisal of the Department of Health research studies in child protection, *Child and Family Social Work*, Vol. 1, No. 1, pp. 3-11.

Parton, N., Thorpe, D. and Wattam, C. (1997), *Child Protection: Risk and the Moral Order*, Macmillan: London.

Price, J. R. (1994), 'Change for change's sake?', *Children UK*, Summer 1994, National Children's Bureau: London.

Pritchard, C. (1992), 'Children's homicide as an indicator of effective child protection: a comparative study of Western European statistics', *British Journal of Social Work*, Vol. 22, pp. 663-84.

Pritchard, C. (1993), 'Re-analysing children's homicide and undetermined death rates as an indication of improved child protection', *British Journal of Social Work*, Vol. 23, No. 6, pp. 645-652.

Reder, P., Duncan, S. and Gray, M. (1993), *Beyond Blame: Child Abuse Tragedies Revisited*, Routledge: London and New York.

Robbins, D. (1990), *Child Care Policy: Putting it in Writing*, HMSO: London.

Robinson, R. and LeGrand, J. (eds.) (1994). *Evaluating the NHS Reforms,* Kings Fund Institute/Policy Journals: Newbury, Berkshire.

Rose, L. (1994), *Working Together for Children's Welfare: Child Protection and the Rôle of the Education System*, Report of the Conference hosted by the Michael Sieff Foundation at Cumberland Lodge, March 1994, Michael Sieff Foundation: Surrey.

Sallis, J. (1988), *Schools, Parents and Governors: A New Approach to Accountability*, Routledge: London.

Sanders, B. (1993), *The Children Act 1989: A Guide for Voluntary Organisations*, Caerphilly, Wales Council for Voluntary Action: Caerphilly, Wales.

Sanders, R., Jackson, S. and Thomas, N. (1996a), 'The Balance of Prevention, Investigation, and Treatment in the Management of Child Protection Services', *Child Abuse & Neglect*, Vol. 20, No. 10, pp. 899-906.

Sanders, R, Jackson, S. and Thomas, N. (1996b), 'The Police Role in the Management of Child Protection Services', *Policing and Society*, Vol. 6, pp. 87-100.

Sanders, R.M., Jackson, S. and Thomas, N. (1996c), 'What is Risk?' Interactive Poster (Abstract 129) presented at IPSCAN Eleventh International Congress on Child Abuse and Neglect, 18-21 August 1996.

Sanders, R.M., Jackson, S. and Thomas, N. (in press), Degrees of Involvement: the Interaction of Focus and Commitment in Area Child Protection Committees, *British Journal of Social Work* (forthcoming).

Secretaries of State (1989), *Working for Patients*, HMSO: London.

Simon, B. and Chitty, C. (1993), *SOS: Save Our Schools*, Lawrence & Wishart: London.

Simpson, C., Simpson, R., Power, K., Salter, A. and Williams, G-J.(1994), 'GPs' and Health Visitors' Participation in Child Protection Case Conferences', *Child Abuse Review*, Vol. 3, pp. 211-30.

Social Services Inspectorate (1995), *Children's Services Plans 1993/94*, HMSO: London.

Social Services Inspectorate/Department of Health (1993*), Inspecting for Quality: Evaluating Performance in Child Protection*, HMSO: London.

Social Services Inspectorate (Wales) (1992), *Accommodating Children*.

Social Services Inspectorate (Wales) (1995), *Preparing Children's Services Plans*.

Social Services Inspectorate (Wales) (1996), *Area Child Protection Committees and Local Government Reorganisation*, March 1996, SSI(W): Cardiff.

Stevenson, O. (1989), *Child Abuse: Public Policy and Professional Practice*, Harvester Wheatsheaf: Hertfordshire.

Thorpe, D. (1994) *Evaluating Child Protection*, Open University Press: Milton Keynes.

Thomas, N. (1994) "The social worker as 'bad object': a response to Marguerite Valentine", *British Journal of Social Work*, Vol. 24, No. 6, pp. 749-54.

Thomas, N. (1995), 'Allegations of child abuse in local authority foster care', *Practice*, Vol 7, No. 3, pp. 35-44.

Tite, R. (1993), 'How teachers define and respond to child abuse: the distinction between theoretical and reportable cases', *Child Abuse and Neglect*, Vol. 17, No. 5, pp. 591-603.

Weightman, K. (1988), 'Managing from below: social work and child abuse', *Social Work Today*, 29 September 1988, pp. 16-17.

Welsh Office Circular (WOC 64/94), *Protection of Children: Disclosure of Criminal Background to Voluntary Sector Organisations*.

Welsh Office Circular (WOC 54/93), *Protection of Children: Disclosure of Criminal Background of those with access to children*.

Welsh Office Circular (WOC 38/93), *Guidance on Permissible Forms of control in children's residential care*.

Welsh Office Circular (WOC 60/95), *Child Protection: Clarification of Arrangements between the NHS and Other Agencies*.

Welsh Office Circular (WOC 35/96), *Child Care Procedures and Practice in North Wales: Implementation of the Report of Ms Adrianne Jones*.

Whitfield, R. (1987), 'Strategies for prevention: education for good child care practice', chapter 9 in Maher, P. (ed.)(1987) *Child Abuse: The Educational Perspective*, Blackwell: Oxford.

Williams, C. (1995), 'Local government reorganisation in Wales: an Update', *Children UK*, Spring 1995, National Children's Bureau: London.

Williams, J. (1992), 'Working Together II', *Journal of Child Law*, April, pp. 68-71.

Williams of Mostyn, Lord (1996), *Childhood Matters; Report of the National Commissison of Inquiry into the Prevention of Child Abuse*, The Stationery Office: London.

Index

children in need, 13, 58, 106, 121, 124, 125, 126, 127, 128, 129, 130, 131, 138

Children in the Public Care (Utting Report), 123

Choosing with Care (Warner Report), 124

Cleveland inquiry report, 5, 46, 64, 75, 107, 112, 125

clinical psychologist, 44

Colwell inquiry report, 4, 52

communities, 58, 109, 110, 128, 136, 137, 138, 139

community, 14, 20, 28, 30, 31, 32, 36, 37, 43, 49, 99, 101, 125, 129, 130, 137, 139

community child health service, 30, 125

complaints, 59, 76, 78, 88, 92, 135

continuing medical education (CME), 27, 34

contract culture, 93, 102

core groups, 76, 78, 88

court, 32

critical incident reporting, 72

Crown Prosecution Service, 44, 66, 90

culture, 4, 91, 93, 102

day care, 122, 125, 128, 138

decentralisation, 95, 99, 110, 117

designated senior doctor, 30

designated senior midwife, 30, 31

designated senior nurse, 30, 31

designated teacher, 27, 36, 37, 38, 97

district health authority, 3

district subcommittee, 25, 45, 49, 53, 62, 64, 65, 66, 67, 73, 100, 105

district subcommittees, 65, 67, 72

domestic violence, 35

education, 1, 4, 10, 16, 17, 21, 26, 27, 34, 36, 37, 38, 39, 42, 44, 49, 51, 52, 53, 54, 61, 63, 64, 93, 94, 95, 96, 97, 98, 100, 103, 104, 110, 117, 122, 124, 125, 127, 130, 135, 138

Education Reform Act 1988, 94

effectiveness, 1, 3, 8, 9, 12, 14, 15, 16, 22, 24, 36, 45, 48, 51, 52, 56, 70, 72, 73, 118, 121, 124, 126, 133, 135, 141

emotional abuse, 5, 21, 82

ethnicity, 91

evaluation, 14, 76, 99, 118

family group conferences, 58, 137

family support, 13, 16, 35, 122, 125, 126, 128

family support unit (police), 36

female genital mutilation, 21, 58, 78, 79, 90, 92

general practitioner, 3, 10, 11, 20, 26, 27, 31, 32, 33, 34, 37, 39, 41, 44, 46, 49, 50, 51, 52, 63, 69, 79, 80, 94, 99, 100, 101, 102, 103, 116

generic vs specialist practice, 13, 21, 26, 27, 28, 30, 32, 35, 36, 49, 89, 91, 106, 107

guidelines, 2, 3, 18, 20, 22, 26, 27, 28, 31, 33, 36, 39, 53, 74, 81

headteacher, 10, 11, 36, 37, 38, 42, 52, 97, 152

health service, 10, 30, 31, 32, 33, 36, 39, 42, 43, 44, 46, 51, 53, 54, 64, 98, 99, 100, 101, 102, 115

health visitor, 31, 32

Home Office, 2, 7, 17, 61, 93

hospital services, 30, 31, 32, 33, 43, 99, 101, 130

housing, 66, 116, 124, 125

independent schools, 74

inquiry, 2, 5, 6, 21, 22, 52, 94, 95, 112, 113, 125, 136

INSET days, 27, 98

investigation, 6, 13, 24, 29, 35, 46, 52, 54, 58, 60, 61, 62, 64, 73, 76, 78, 81, 82, 84, 86, 92, 94, 95, 105, 115, 118, 121, 125, 134, 135, 136, 142

163

involvement (agencies), 42, 62
involvement (parental), 57, 58, 73, 76, 84, 85, 133, 143
involvement (the child), 76, 86

Johnson inquiry report, 52
joint investigation (police/social work), 76, 78, 81, 92

language, 77, 86, 87, 91, 92, 94
legal procedures, 2
local education authority, 3, 11, 26, 31, 36, 38, 42, 44, 51, 63, 94, 95, 96, 97
Local Government (Wales) Act 1994, 103
local government reorganisation, 14, 17, 28, 54, 65, 94, 103, 104, 106, 108, 109, 110
local management of schools (LMS), 36, 95, 96
local medical committee (LMC), 3, 33, 34, 50
Looking After Children (LAC), 14

management information systems, 71, 72
management structure, 27, 28, 30, 32, 33, 44
managers, 2, 3, 15, 18, 21, 24, 26, 29, 30, 40, 42, 45, 48, 49, 52, 53, 66, 75, 101, 107, 108, 121, 134, 136
media, 59, 65, 89, 91, 92, 109, 111, 113, 118, 133
Memorandum of Good Practice, 16, 61, 90
middle managers, 40, 66
midwife, 30, 31
monitoring, 2, 14, 31, 32, 58, 64, 66, 69, 70, 71, 72, 113, 116, 117, 118, 121, 123, 124, 129, 138, 144

National Association for the Development of Work with Sex Offenders (NOTA), 21

national curriculum, 39, 94
National Health Service and Community Care Act 1990, 94, 99
National Health Service trusts, 43, 99, 100
National Society for the Prevention of Cruelty to Children (NSPCC), 3, 10, 21, 31, 44, 52, 66, 95, 108, 138
NCH Action for Children, 52, 108
neglect, 4, 5, 21, 47, 65, 81, 82, 91, 111, 131, 138
NHS trusts, 25, 31
non-accidental injury, 5
North America, 4, 38
North Wales Inquiry, 6, 17, 25, 109
nurses, 31, 32, 42
nursing, 3, 11, 32, 33, 42

organised abuse, 6, 22, 58, 89, 90, 91

paediatrician, 10, 11, 44, 66, 80, 102
parental criminality, 116
parental delinquency, 116
parental psychiatric disorder, 113
part 8 reviews, 3, 6, 14, 20, 21, 65, 71, 88, 91, 94, 111, 112, 113, 115, 116, 117, 118, 119, 120, 132, 153
physical abuse, 20, 21, 81
Pindown scandal (Staffordshire), 123
police, 5, 10, 17, 18, 29, 35, 36, 38, 39, 42, 43, 44, 45, 50, 51, 52, 53, 54, 55, 58, 61, 62, 63, 64, 68, 74, 76, 81, 82, 83, 87, 93, 100, 105, 107, 108, 109, 113, 116, 117
police surgeon, 44
policy (child protection), 3, 6, 8, 9, 14, 15, 16, 17, 19, 22, 29, 34, 36, 37, 38, 39, 60, 61, 69, 74, 76, 92, 98, 132, 134, 136, 142
practitioners, 9, 13, 15, 18, 21, 24, 25, 26, 27, 28, 29, 33, 34, 40, 42, 49, 51, 53, 65, 69, 74, 75, 78, 79, 80, 81, 82, 86, 98, 99, 116, 134, 135, 136, 139